Excel

ADVANCED SKILLS

ENGLISH

YEAR 2

AGES 7–8

SPELLING AND VOCABULARY WORKBOOK

Get the Results You Want!

PASCAL PRESS

Donna Gibbs

Reprinted 2015, 2016, 2017, 2019, 2020, 2021, 2022

Updated in 2025 for the NSW Curriculum and Australian Curriculum Version 9.0 changes

ISBN 978 1 74125 465 5

Pascal Press
PO Box 250
Glebe NSW 2037
www.pascalpress.com.au

Publisher: Vivienne Joannou
Series developer: Kristine Brown
Project editors: Mark Dixon and Leanne Poll
Edited by Leanne Howard
Reviewed by Dale Little
Typeset by Grizzly Graphics (Leanne Richters)
Cover and page design by DiZign Pty Ltd
Printed by Vivar Printing/Green Giant Press

Contents

To the student

Winnie the Pooh thought he was a good speller. It was just that some of the letters got out of order! The problem is that to be a good speller, all letters have to be in the correct order.

You can learn to be a good speller. There are rules for spelling words and there are spelling patterns that match sound patterns. This book will show you some of those patterns and teach you some of those rules. It will even teach you clever tricks to help you remember long words and words that don't fit the rules.

You will need a dictionary (the *Macquarie Junior Dictionary* if possible) and a sharp pencil. You will also need a quiet place to work with good light so you don't strain your eyes. You will be able to do the exercises in this book all by yourself if you have all those things.

It will also be a big help if you have an adult or big brother or sister to hear you spell the words once you think you know them. When you spell a word aloud to someone else, it stays in your brain much longer than if you just spell it to yourself.

You can't write well without good spelling. When you have finished this book, you will be well on the way to becoming a good writer.

You'll also find fun puzzles using the words from each unit. There are crosswords, wordsearches and other word games. There are jokes and riddles at the end of each unit that use the words you are learning.

I hope you enjoy working through the book. Good luck and have fun!

LOOK-SAY-COVER-WRITE-SAY-CHECK method

The **LOOK-SAY-COVER-WRITE-SAY-CHECK** method is always useful for learning to spell words. Follow these steps:

- **LOOK** at the word.
  What does it mean? What shapes do the letters make? What other words is it spelt like? Underline any hard parts.
- **SAY** the word aloud.
  Listen to the sounds in the word. Clap out its syllables. Spell it.
- **COVER** the word.
  Get ready to write it down.
- **WRITE** the word without looking back at it.
- **SAY** the word out loud again to check that you have remembered its sounds and spelling correctly.
- **CHECK** that the spelling is correct.
  If you get it right, write it once more. If you get it wrong, use the **LOOK-SAY-COVER-WRITE-SAY-CHECK method** again.

1 What can my body do?

Quick fun

Fill in the missing letters to spell the words from the box.
The first one has been done for you.

smell	hear
see	watch
walk	look

1. s e e
2. l__ __ __
3. w__ __ __ __
4. h__ __ __
5. s__ __ __ __
6. w__ __ __

Topic spelling list

Use the **LOOK-SAY-COVER-WRITE-SAY-CHECK** strategy to learn these words.

see	look	watch
stare	hear	listen
breathe	smell	sniff
taste	whisper	talk
yell	move	lift
bend	walk	run

Use this space to write out your topic words the first time. Use your own paper for extra practice.

Rewrite here those you had the most trouble with.

Spelling strategy

LOOK-SAY-COVER-WRITE-SAY-CHECK method

LOOK-SAY-COVER-WRITE-SAY-CHECK is a plan for learning to spell words. (You can check this out on page 1 at the beginning of this book.)

1. **LOOK** at the word.
2. **SAY** the word and listen to its sounds.
3. **COVER** the word.
4. **WRITE** the word.
5. **SAY** the word and listen to its sounds again.
6. **CHECK** that the spelling is correct.

Choose six of the most challenging words from the **Topic Spelling list** and write them in Column 1 below. Then use the LOOK-SAY-COVER-WRITE-SAY-CHECK method to learn and practise their spellings.

1				
2				
3				
4				
5				
6				

Fill in the gaps

Choose words from the **Topic spelling list** to complete these sentences. The first one has been done for you.

1. Do not walk ________________ on the grass.
2. I b________________ through my nose.
3. Did you s________________ her win the race?
4. If you r________________ you move your legs quickly.
5. If you t________________ you speak words out loud.
6. If you w________________ you speak very softly.

Tricky words

Some words are spelt and sound the same, but have different meanings. Find the words from the **Topic spelling list** that have these different meanings.

1. a look at something for some time

   b a small clock worn on your arm

   The word is: ____________________

2. a a turn in the road

   b move something so it isn't straight

   The word is: ____________________

3. a move to a higher place

   b something you travel inside to move up or down

   The word is: ____________________

Looking at ... vowels and consonants

There are five letters in the alphabet called **vowels**: ***a, e, i, o*** and ***u***. Think of a way to remember them.
For example: the sentence ***A****nn's* ***E****gg* ***I****s* ***O****n* ***U****s*.

Letters in the alphabet that are not vowels are called **consonants**. There are 21 consonants in the alphabet. They are ***b, c, d, f, g, h, j, k, l, m, n, p, q, r, s, t, v, w, x, y*** and ***z***.

How many vowels and consonants are there in these words? The first one has been done for you.

	Word	How many vowels (Vs)?	How many consonants (Cs)?
1	hear	2 Vs	2 Cs
2	stare		
3	walk		
4	listen		
5	breathe		

Proofreading

Find five spelling mistakes and write the words correctly below. The first one has been done for you.

I heer a loud noise. What can it be? I wark to the window and stair out. Now I sea what made the noise. The cat rann away from the dog and crashed into the rubbish bin.

1 hear
2 ______
3 ______
4 ______
5 ______

Vocabulary power

Action (doing) verbs tell you what is happening. They describe all the different actions people, animals and things do.
For example: *run, listen* and *move.*

Find action (doing) verbs from the box that rhyme with those in the columns. The first one has been done for you.

cook	dump
paste	mend
waste	bump
send	took

jump	taste	bend	look
dump			

Read and learn

Read the text below. What do the words in **bold** mean?

I learn hip hop dancing. We **copy** the actions of our teacher. **Sometimes** the music goes so **quickly** I can't keep up. Then I start to **giggle**. But my teacher laughs too. So we try **again** to get it right.

Circle the answer closest in meaning to the word in **bold**.
The first one has been done for you.

1 **copy**	a choose	b do the same as	c draw
2 **Sometimes**	a always	b often	c now and then
3 **quickly**	a slow	b fast	c loudly
4 **giggle**	a yawn	b wriggle	c laugh
5 **again**	a another time	b once	c also

Puzzle

Draw the answers to these puzzles.

1 I walk, jump and run. I rhyme with *pegs*. What am I?	2 I sniff, smell and blow. I rhyme with *hose*. What am I?
3 I see, look and watch. I rhyme with *pies*. What am I?	4 I touch, hold and grip. I rhyme with *bands*. What am I?
5 I taste, talk and eat. I rhyme with *south*. What am I?	

Tip!
The answers are all parts of the body.

Your turn to write

Write about things you like to smell, taste and see by completing these sentences. The first one has been done for you. At the end of your writing, add a picture of you doing one of these things.

Revise and edit your work. Check the spelling.
Make a published copy for your teacher, parent or friend.

I like to smell ___cakes cooking___.

I like to smell ______________.

I like to smell ______________.

I like to taste ______________.

I like to taste ______________.

I like to taste ______________.

I like to look at ______________.

I like to look at ______________.

I like to look at ______________.

Reading for fun

✦ **Why was the nose tired?**

Because it kept running.

✦ **What colour is a burp?**

Burple.

✦ **Why couldn't the snake talk?**

He had a frog in his throat.

✦ **What did one eye say to the other?**

Between you and me, something smells.

☞ Answers on page 108

2 Plenty of places

Quick fun

Write the words from the box in alphabetical order. The first one has been done for you.

town
city
country
home
desert
mountain

1 city
2 ______
3 ______
4 ______
5 ______
6 ______

Topic spelling list

Use the **LOOK-SAY-COVER-WRITE-SAY-CHECK** strategy to learn these words.

city	country	town
village	beach	river
lake	island	home
desert	oasis	garden
mountain	valley	plain
park	playground	supermarket

Use this space to write out your topic words the first time. Use your own paper for extra practice.

Rewrite here those you had the most trouble with.

Spelling strategy

Little words in big words

Some words have other words hidden inside them.
For example: ***city*** has the word ***it*** inside it. This can help you remember its spelling.

Find a word hidden inside these words. The first one has been done for you.

1. beach ____each____
2. park ________
3. garden ________
4. island ________
5. oasis ________
6. plain ________

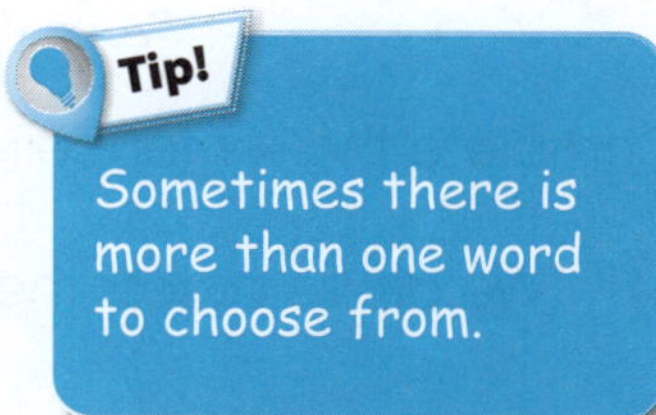

Fill in the gaps

Using the clues to help you, choose words from the **Topic spelling list** to complete these sentences. The first one has been done for you.

1. This is a r _i_ v _e_ r where I swim.
2. Here is the pl__ __g__ __ __ __d near our house.
3. He climbed a very high m__ __nt__ __n.
4. We are going to the __ __a __h on the weekend.
5. We shop at the s__ __ __r__ __r__ __ __ on Thursdays.
6. These are sunflowers in our __ar__ __ __.

Tricky words

The words ***plain*** and ***plane*** sound the same but have different meanings and spellings. Think of a way to remember the difference.
For example: you need a ***plan*** to build a ***plane***.

Word	Meaning	Example
plain	large area of flat land	*We flew over a* ***plain****.*
plane	machine that can fly	*We flew in a* ***plane*** *to Perth.*

Complete the sentences with the correct word (*plain* or *plane*).

1. We drove across the ____________________.
2. Are you going by ____________________?
3. His dad is building a ____________________.
4. There aren't any trees on that ____________________.

Looking at…short and long vowels

Short vowels make a short sound.
For example: *p**a**t, p**e**t, p**i**t, p**o**t* and *p**u**t*.

Long vowels make a long sound. Some are made with two vowels side by side. They often sound like the name of their letter.
For example: *p**a**le, p**ee**l, p**i**le, p**o**le, p**oo**l* and *p**u**re*.

Do the **bold** vowels in these words make a **short** or a **long** sound? The first one has been done for you.

	Word	Short or long vowel
1	sh**o**p	short
2	h**o**me	
3	r**i**ver	
4	v**a**lley	
5	l**a**ke	
6	isl**a**nd	

Proofreading

Find six spelling mistakes and write the words correctly below. The first one has been done for you.

I'd like to see Mownt Fuji in Japan won day.

Another plase I want to vizit is Disneyland.

I'd also like to ride a camel across the dessert.

I'd find an oasiss and have a drink of water.

1. Mount
2. ______
3. ______
4. ______
5. ______
6. ______

Vocabulary power

Particular places are always spelt with **capital letters**.
For example: ***B****risbane,* ***C****radle* ***M****ountain,* ***L****una* ***P****ark* and ***H****illtop* ***P****rimary.*

There are five words with missing capital letters in this text. Write the words correctly on the lines below. The first one has been done for you.

Tom: We're going to bondi beach. Want to come?

Tim: I can't. Dad is taking us to the city today.

Tom: You mean to sydney?

Tim: Yes, but tomorrow we are going to shark island. Want to come?

Tom: Yes, please!

1. Bondi
2. ______
3. ______
4. ______
5. ______

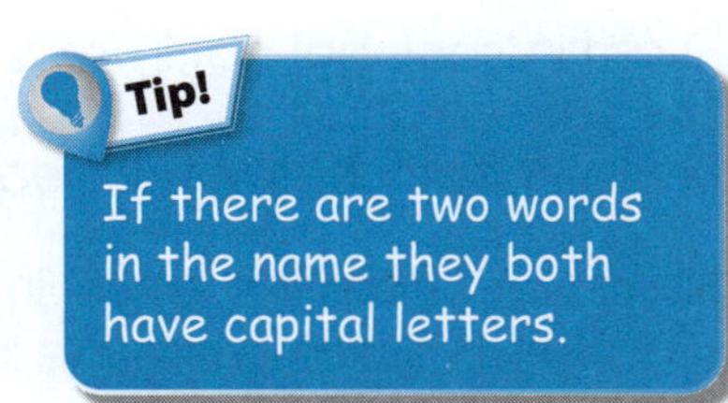

Tip!

If there are two words in the name they both have capital letters.

Read and learn

Read the text below. What do the words in **bold** mean?

Uluru is a rock on a **dry** desert plain in the middle of Australia. The rock is **gigantic**. It is more than 3 km in **length** and over 9 km around. The First Nations people of Australia are its **owners**. You can **visit** their rock paintings at Uluru.

Circle the answer closest in meaning to the word in **bold**. The first one has been done for you.

1 **dry**	a clean	b hot	c without much water
2 **gigantic**	a big	b huge	c middle sized
3 **length**	a long	b tall	c high
4 **owners**	a users	b keepers	c painters
5 **visit**	a go to hear	b go to touch	c go to see

Puzzle

1 Answer the questions with a letter of the alphabet.

What am I?

- I am in *send* but not in *sand*. ____________
- I am in *hill* but not in *pill*. ____________
- I am in *turn* but not in *torn*. ____________
- I am in *sock* but not in *rock*. ____________
- I am in *boat* but not in *beat*. ____________

2 Make a word from the letters in your answers that names a building people live in. ____________

Your turn to write

Describe a place that you like to visit. Where is it? What kind of place is it? What do you like about it? At the end of your description, add a picture of your place.

Revise and edit your work. Check the spelling. Make a published copy for your teacher, parent or friend.

Title: ______________________________

Reading for fun

- **Why did the chicken cross the playground?**
  To get to the other slide.
- **How do fleas travel from place to place?**
  By itch-hiking.
- **What should you take on a trip to the desert?**
  A thirst-aid kit.

☞ Answers on page 108

3 Did you hear that?

Quick fun

Unscramble the letters to make the words in the box. The first one has been done for you.

chirp
snarl
hoot
fizz
knock
croak

1. rkaoc ______ croak
2. thoo ______
3. zifz ______
4. cknok ______
5. pirhc ______
6. larns ______

Topic spelling list

Use the **LOOK-SAY-COVER-WRITE-SAY-CHECK** strategy to learn these words.

bang	chime	chirp
chuckle	crash	croak
crunch	fizz	groan
hoot	howl	knock
rustle	roar	rumble
sizzle	snarl	whistle

Use this space to write out your topic words the first time. Use your own paper for extra practice.

Rewrite here those you had the most trouble with.

Spelling strategy

Learn a spelling rule: words ending in *e*

A spelling rule to remember is that words that end in the letter ***e*** drop the ***e*** before adding more letters to make a new word.
For example: when we add ***ing*** to the word ***make*** we get ***making***.

Make some new words by adding ***ing*** to the words listed below. The first one has been done for you.

1 chime	chiming	5 chuckle	
2 howl		6 groan	
3 roar		7 crunch	
4 sizzle		8 whistle	

Fill in the gaps

Choose words from the **Topic spelling list** to complete these sentences. The first one has been done for you.

Did you hear the:

1. sausage ____sizzle____?
2. lion ________________?
3. owl ________________?
4. frog ________________?
5. bells ________________?
6. thunder ________________?

Tricky words

Some words have consonants that stay silent when you say them. This makes them tricky to spell. For example: the word ***knife*** has a silent ***k*** and the word ***listen*** has a silent ***t***.

1. Find a word in the **Topic spelling list** that has a silent ***k***. ______________________

2. Find two words in the **Topic spelling list** that have a silent ***t***.

   ______________________ ______________________

3. Now it's time to go fishing. Jimmy wants to catch fish that have words with silent letters inside them. Help Jimmy by circling these fish for him.

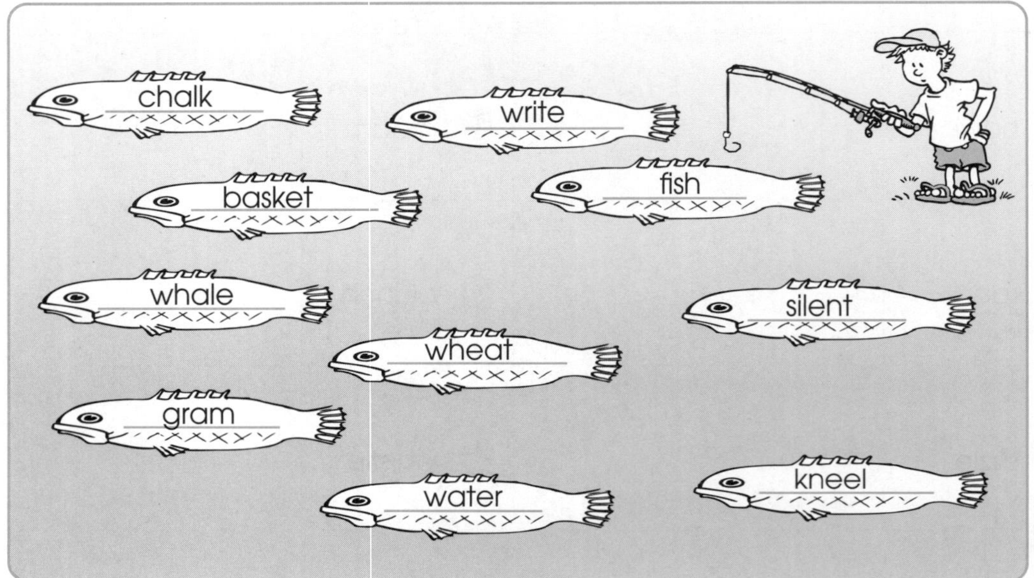

Looking at…short vowel sounds

Remember that **short vowels** make a short sound. They are often spelt with a single vowel (*a, e, i, o* and *u*). Underline the short vowels in these words from the **Topic spelling list**. The first one has been done for you.

1. ch u ckle
2. bang
3. knock
4. rustle
5. fizz
6. sizzle

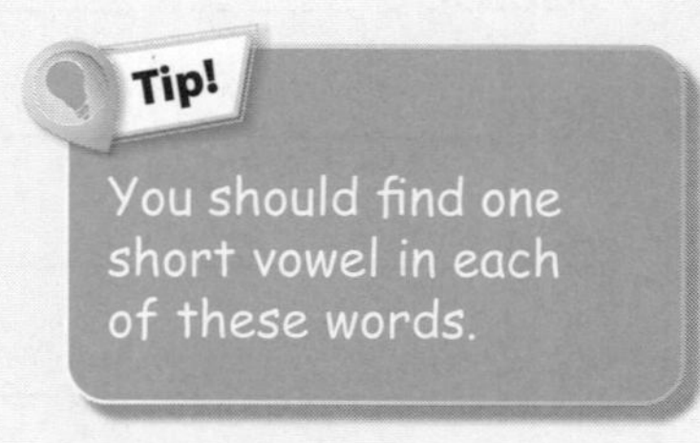

Proofreading

Find five spelling mistakes and write the words correctly below. The first one has been done for you.

What makes a noise at your howse? The birds cherp and whisle in the mornings. Our fridge makes a soft, rumling sownd. The phone rings loudly. Even I make a lot of noise sometimes!

1. house
2. ____________________
3. ____________________
4. ____________________
5. ____________________

Vocabulary power

Repeating a sound at the beginning of words is called **alliteration**.
For example: the ***r**ed **r**obot **r**oared **r**udely* repeats the ***r*** sound. This can make things sound scary, funny, sad, etc.

Link words from column 1 with words beginning with the same sound in column 2. Say the words aloud to check you have the right pair. The first one has been done for you.

	Column 1	**Column 2**
1	whirring	goats
2	exercising	neighbours
3	sizzling	elephants
4	giggling	yaks
5	yowling	wheels
6	noisy	sausages

Read and learn

Read the text below. What do the words in **bold** mean?

My sisters and I have a **band**. We make music **together**. We're not **famous** yet! We invite our family and friends to **listen** to us. Once, when we played a soft **lullaby**, Mum fell asleep and snored!

Circle the answer closest in meaning to the word in **bold**. The first one has been done for you.

		a	b	c
1	**band**	piece of rubber	(group who plays music)	bangle
2	**together**	always	with each other	apart
3	**famous**	well-known	important	great
4	**listen**	hear	watch	see
5	**lullaby**	anthem	nursery rhyme	soothing song

Puzzle

Draw a line from the sound to the picture that makes that sound.

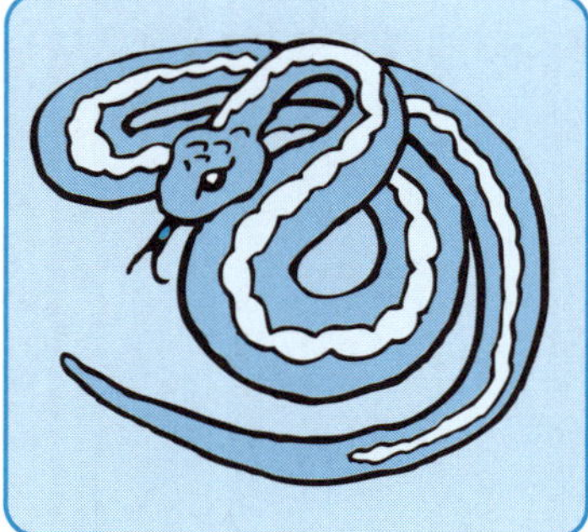

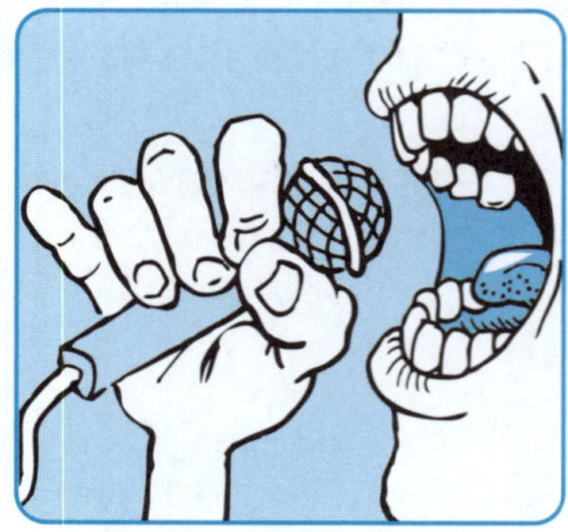

Tick tock

Ssssss

Baaaa baaaaa

Boo hoo

La la la la

Your turn to write

Write a story about a strange noise. Choose a title. Who heard the strange noise? Where did it come from? What did it sound like? What happened? At the end of your story, add a picture.

Revise and edit your work. Check the spelling. Make a published copy for your teacher, parent or friend.

Title: ______________________________

____

____

____

____

____

____

____

____

____

____

____

____

Reading for fun

Tongue twisters are strings of words that are hard to say quickly. The pattern of their sounds can trip up your tongue. Say these quickly ten times each.

Selfish shellfish.

Soldier's shoulders.

Crisp crusts crackle and crunch

 ☞ Answers on pages 108–109

4 Colours and shapes

Quick fun

Find words from the **Topic spelling list** to rhyme with these words. The first one has been done for you.

1. seen rhymes with green
2. sink rhymes with ______
3. sack rhymes with______
4. who rhymes with ______
5. hair rhymes with ______
6. ate rhymes with ______

Topic spelling list

Use the **LOOK-SAY-COVER-WRITE-SAY-CHECK** strategy to learn these words.

black	white	red
blue	green	pink
brown	orange	purple
yellow	square	circle
spiral	rectangle	triangle
oval	straight	curved

Use this space to write out your topic words the first time. Use your own paper for extra practice.

Rewrite here those you had the most trouble with.

Spelling strategy

LOOK-SAY-COVER-WRITE-SAY-CHECK method

Choose six of the most challenging words from the **Topic Spelling list** and write them in Column 1 below. Then use the LOOK-SAY-COVER-WRITE-SAY-CHECK method to learn and practise their spellings.

1				
2				
3				
4				
5				
6				

Fill in the gaps

Choose words from the **Topic spelling list** to complete these sentences. The first one has been done for you.

1. A r<u>ectangle</u>__________ is an oblong shape.
2. Bananas are y______________________.
3. I ruled a s______________________ line.
4. A c______________________ is a round shape.
5. White is the opposite of b______________________.
6. A t______________________ is a shape with three sides.

Tricky words

Some words are spelt and sound the same, but have different meanings. Find the words from the **Topic spelling list** that have both these meanings.

1. a a round, juicy fruit

   b a colour between red and yellow

   The word is: ____________________

2. a shaped like an egg

   b a field where you play games

   The word is: ____________________

3. a an open space in a city where people meet

   b a shape with four straight sides of the same length

   The word is: ____________________

Looking at … silent letter *e*

The letter ***e*** is often silent when it comes at the end of a word.
For example: the word *purpl**e*** ends with the letter ***e*** but when you say the word you hear an ***l*** sound.

Choose a word from the box ending with a silent ***e*** to describe the following. The first one has been done for you.

triangle	pale
whole	rectangle
bundle	circle

1. a round shape ______circle______
2. a shape with four straight sides ____________________
3. a shape with three sides ____________________
4. a group of things held together ____________________
5. light in colour ____________________
6. the full amount ____________________

Proofreading

Find five spelling mistakes and write the words correctly below. The first one has been done for you.

I know how to make grean paint. First I get some blew paint. Then I get some yelow paint. Using a paintbrush, I mix the collours together. Then I use it to paint tres and grass.

1. green
2. __________
3. __________
4. __________
5. __________

Vocabulary power

Some sayings don't really make sense, yet people understand them. These sayings are called **idioms**.

For example: the saying "Tom's the black sheep of the family" means the family thinks Tom has let them down. Of course, he is not a black sheep!

Link the sentences to their meanings. The first one has been done for you.

	Sentences	**Meanings**
1	I was caught red-handed with the biscuit tin.	I went pale with shock.
2	I went as white as a sheet.	I looked crossly at him.
3	I was tickled pink with my present.	I'm not getting anywhere.
4	I'm going round in circles.	I was very pleased with my present.
5	I gave him a black look.	I was caught opening the biscuit tin.

Read and learn

Read the text below. What do the words in **bold** mean?

> There are spiral shapes **everywhere**.
> A staircase that goes around and **around** makes a spiral **shape**. So does a thumbprint.
> Water **swirls** down a plughole in a spiral shape. What **else** has this shape?

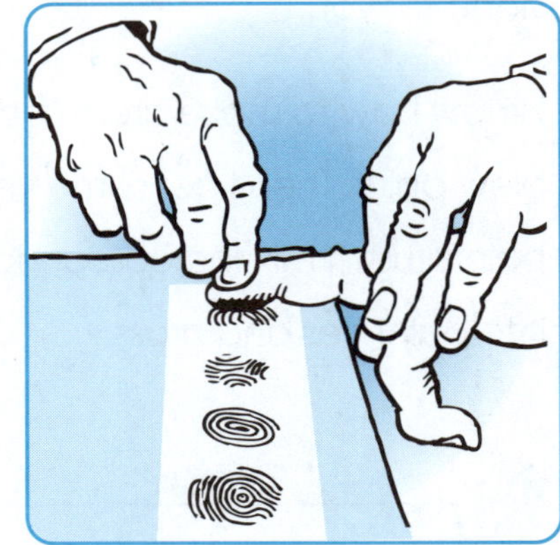

Circle the answer closest in meaning to the word in **bold**. The first one has been done for you.

1 **everywhere**	a somewhere	b in all places (circled)	c over here
2 **around**	a down	b across	c in circles
3 **shape**	a picture	b form	c circle
4 **swirls**	a whirls	b tips	c falls
5 **else**	a here	b more	c there

Puzzle

Find these words in the word search puzzle below. Words go across and down.

- red
- purple
- circle
- white
- square
- black

r	s	w	e	m	w	l
b	t	h	i	p	h	k
l	o	p	d	d	i	s
a	v	u	c	a	t	q
c	i	r	c	l	e	u
k	a	p	l	s	t	a
r	x	l	y	b	e	r
u	r	e	d	a	l	e

Your turn to write

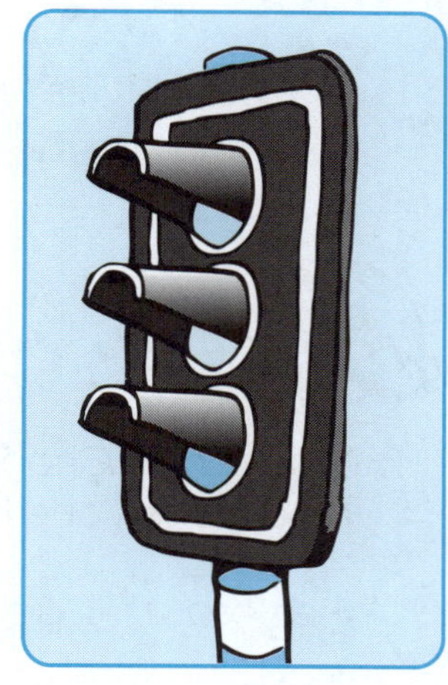

Write down what to do when crossing the road at traffic lights. What do you do first? What do you do next? Then what? Anything else? At the end of your instructions, add a picture of people at traffic lights.

Revise and edit your work. Check the spelling. Make a published copy for your teacher, parent or friend.

Title: How to cross the road at the traffic lights

Reading for fun

- **What's a cat's favourite colour?**
  Puuuuuurple.

- **What's bright blue and very heavy?**
  An elephant holding its breath.

- **What did the triangle say to the circle?**
  "You're pointless."

☞ Answers on page 109

5 Reporting on reptiles

Quick fun

What am I? Choose an answer from the box. The first one has been done for you.

dinosaur	gecko	crocodile
turtle	snake	

1. I have long jaws and short legs.
   I am a *crocodile*.
2. I have a shell and swim in the sea.
   I am a ____________________.
3. I haven't any legs or eyelids.
   I am a ____________________.
4. I am a small lizard.
   I am a ____________________.
5. I lived millions of years ago.
   I am a ____________________.

Use this space to write out your topic words the first time. Use your own paper for extra practice.

Rewrite here those you had the most trouble with.

Topic spelling list

Use the **LOOK-SAY-COVER-WRITE-SAY-CHECK** strategy to learn these words.

slide	glide	slither
swim	scaly	shell
ear holes	fangs	jaws
skin	tail	alligator
snake	lizard	turtle
crocodile	dinosaur	gecko

Spelling strategy

LOOK-SAY-COVER-WRITE-SAY-CHECK method

Choose six of the most challenging words from the **Topic Spelling list** and write them in Column 1 below. Then use the LOOK-SAY-COVER-WRITE-SAY-CHECK method to learn and practise their spellings.

1				
2				
3				
4				
5				
6				

Fill in the gaps

Choose words from the **Topic spelling list** to complete these sentences. The first one has been done for you.

1. The snake's ____fangs____ are poisonous.
2. That dinosaur has a very long ____________.
3. Crocodiles have ____________ skin.
4. Alligators like to ____________ in rivers.
5. A turtle has a ____________ on its back.
6. I saw a snake ____________ into the bushes.

Tricky words

The words ***hole*** and ***whole*** sound the same but have different meanings and spellings.
Think of a way to remember the difference.
For example: say the ***wh**ole **w**ide **w**orld* to yourself to remember which *whole* begins with a ***w***.

Word	Meaning	Example
hole	an opening	*There is a **hole** in my pocket.*
whole	all of something	*I ate the **whole** of my lunch.*

Complete the sentences with the correct spelling (*hole* or *whole*).

1. The snake swallowed a ____________________ frog.
2. Spot dug a ____________________ for his bone.
3. The gecko hid in a ____________________ in the wall.
4. I ran the ____________________ way home.

Looking at … split digraphs

Split digraphs are formed when a consonant comes between two vowels (e.g. ***a*** and ***e***; ***i*** and ***e***). An ***e*** on the end of a word often gives a long sound to the vowel before it. For example: the ***a*** sound in ***scale*** and ***pale*** is made long by the ***e*** ending and the ***i*** sound in ***wipe*** and ***stripe*** is made long by the ***e*** ending.

There are eight sweets in the jar with words written on their wrappers. Some of the words have long ***a*** sounds and some have long ***i*** sounds. Sort them into their correct jars.

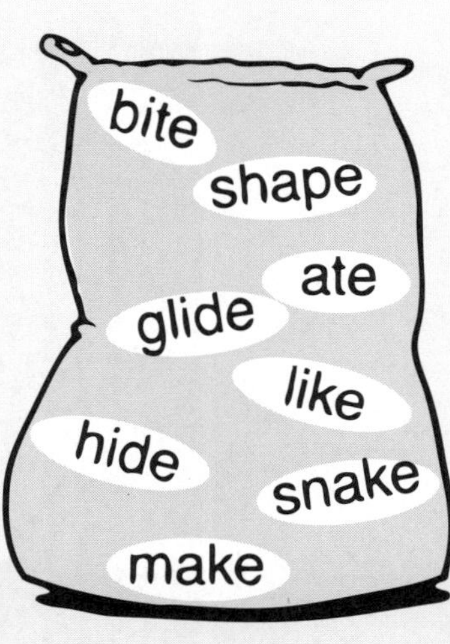

Proofreading

Find six spelling mistakes and write the words correctly below. The first one has been done for you.

Manny years ago, dinosores lived on earth.
Most hatched from egs. Some warked on
two legs. Others used all four legs.
Some had very long tales and were as
big as a huge bilding!

1 Many
2 ______
3 ______
4 ______
5 ______
6 ______

Vocabulary power

An **antonym** is a word opposite in meaning to another word.
For example: ***good*** is the opposite of ***bad***, and ***hot*** is the opposite of ***cold***.

Adrian's information about reptiles is all incorrect! Choose an antonym from the box to replace the underlined words and correct the information. The first one has been done for you.

hard	long	short
cold	scaly	round

1 Turtles have long legs. short
2 Dinosaurs had short necks. ______
3 Reptiles are hot-blooded animals. ______
4 The turtle has a very soft shell. ______
5 Crocodiles have smooth skins. ______
6 Snakes have a flat body. ______

Read and learn

Read the text below. What do the words in **bold** mean?

> Reptiles have ear holes **instead** of ears. Their skins are dry and **scaly**. They either have four legs or **no** legs at all. **Some** move along slowly. Others move quickly. Some **glide** to where they want to go.

Circle the answer closest in meaning to the word in **bold**. The first one has been done for you.

1 **instead**	(a in place)	b and	c without
2 **scaly**	a stripy	b covered in scales	c spotty
3 **no**	a not any	b some	c lots of
4 **Some**	a a number of them	b none of them	c all of them
5 **glide**	a move fast	b bump along	c move smoothly

Puzzle

What are these imaginary reptiles? The first one has been done for you.

1. A **snazard** is half s n a k e and half l i z a r d.
2. A **dinodile** is half _ _ _ _ _ _ _ _ _ _ and half _ _ _ _ _ _ _ _ _ _ _ _.
3. A **turtosaur** is half _ _ _ _ _ _ _ _ and half _ _ _ _ _ _ _ _ _ _ _.
4. A **gecktle** is half _ _ _ _ _ _ _ and half _ _ _ _ _ _ _ _.
5. A **lizigator** is half _ _ _ _ _ _ _ _ and half _ _ _ _ _ _ _ _ _ _ _ _ _.
6. A dragon is an imaginary reptile. Look for pictures of dragons in books. Then draw your own dragon in the space below.

Title: My dragon

Your turn to write

Find out all you can about a reptile of your choice. Write the information down in dot point form. At the end of your information, add a picture of your reptile. Revise and edit your work. Check the spelling. Make a published copy for your teacher, parent or friend.

Title: ______________________________

____

____

____

____

____

____

____

Reading for fun

- **What did the snake give to his wife?**
  A goodnight hiss.
- **What is a crocodile's favourite card game?**
  Snap.
- **Why did the dinosaur paint his feet yellow?**
  So he could hide upside-down in the custard.

☞ Answers on page 109

Review 1

Now let's see what you remember of the words you learnt in Units 1–5. There are six tests in this review. You could do them all in one session, or you could break them up and do them over a few days.

Step 1 Look at each group of words in the test to revise the spellings.

Step 2 Cover the five words up and test yourself (column 2). Try to do all five words in one go.

Step 3 Write your score out of 5 in the box. If you got any words wrong, go back and study them again.

Step 4 If possible, ask someone to test you on the words later—an hour or even a day later (column 3).

Test 1

Study	Test yourself	Test with another person
breathe hear listen watch whisper	/5	/5
sniff stare talk taste walk	/5	/5
garden mountain playground school shops	/5	/5
	Total score = out of 15	Total score = out of 15

Test 2

Study	Test yourself	Test with another person
desert island oasis plain valley	/5	/5
beach city country river village	/5	/5
rumble rustle crunch knock sizzle	/5	/5
snarl whistle chuckle crash groan	/5	/5
	Total score = out of 20	Total score = out of 20

Test 3

Study	Test yourself	Test with another person
howl roar rectangle spiral straight	/5	/5
circle purple square triangle white	/5	/5
glide scaly shell slide walk	/5	/5
crocodile dinosaur lizard snake turtle	/5	/5
	Total score = out of 20	Total score = out of 20

Test 4

Write the **bold** words correctly. An example has been done for you. Count your score when you have finished the test.

Spelling mistakes	Correct words	Score ✓ ✗
The school bell **chimmed** loudly.	chimed	
1 They were lost in the **dessert**.		
2 We flew to Perth in a **plain**.		
3 There's a huge **whole** in my jumper.		
4 We are going to climb that **mountian**.		
5 Did you see the **gekko**?		
	Total score	/ 5

Test 5

Which is the **silent letter** in these words? An example has been done for you. Count your score when you have finished the test.

Word	Silent letter	Score ✓ ✗
walk	l	
1 whisper		
2 climb		
3 grumble		
4 listen		
5 knock		
	Total score	/ 5

Test 6

Correct these sentences by circling the letters that should be **capitals**. An example has been done for you.

Sentences	Score ✓ ✗
Can we go to (l)una (p)ark today?	
1 sydney is a capital city.	
2 We had a holiday on kangaroo island.	
3 Have you seen uluru at sunset?	
4 My new school is called palmer primary.	
5 We live in australia.	
Total score	/ 5

Grand total	
Test 1	
Test 2	
Test 3	
Test 4	
Test 5	
Test 6	
Total	/ 70

☞ Answers on page 109

6 Come and play

Quick fun

Put the words from the box in alphabetical order. The first one has been done for you.

1 chess
2 ______
3 ______
4 ______
5 ______
6 ______

football
cricket
rounders
tag
chess
netball

Use this space to write out your topic words the first time. Use your own paper for extra practice.

Topic spelling list

Use the **LOOK-SAY-COVER-WRITE-SAY-CHECK** strategy to learn these words.

ball	swing	slippery dip
netball	rounders	cricket
football	skipping	running
hidey	tag	hopscotch
jigsaw	puzzle	cards
chess	Snakes and Ladders	Snap

Rewrite here those you had the most trouble with.

Spelling strategy

Breaking words into syllables

A **syllable** is a unit of sound within a word. One syllable makes one beat. You can clap the beats to find how many there are in a word.
For example: the words ***dip*** and ***tag*** get one clap each. They are one-syllable words.
The words ***cricket*** and ***football*** get two claps each. They are two-syllable words.
The words ***difficult*** and ***favourite*** get three claps each. They are three-syllable words.
Four claps make four syllables, and so on.

Write the number of syllables that are in each word. The first one has been done for you.

	Word	**How many syllables?**		**Word**	**How many syllables?**
1	netball	two	6	hopping	
2	swing		7	athletic	
3	exercise		8	puzzle	
4	and		9	basketball	
5	jigsaw		10	hopscotch	

Fill in the gaps

Choose words from the **Topic spelling list** to complete these sentences. The first one has been done for you.

1. I slipped down the s<u>lippery dip</u>.
2. She loves s____________ with her new rope.
3. You need a bat to play c____________ and r____________.
4. My brother and I have r____________ races at the park.
5. C____________ is a board game.
6. S____________ is a card game.

Tricky words

Apostrophes (') show where letters are left out. This means that the word ***we're***, spelt with an apostrophe ('), is short for ***we are***.

The words ***we're*** and ***where*** sound the same but have different meanings and spellings. Think what the apostrophe means to remember their differences.

Word	Meaning	Example
we're	we are	***We're*** *going to play netball now.*
where	place you are talking or asking about	***Where*** *did you put the football?*

Underline the correct word, *we're* or *where*, in these sentences.

1. (We're/where) going on a bear hunt.
2. The ball is (we're/where) you kicked it.
3. I don't know (we're/where) I put my sports uniform.
4. (We're/Where) is the last jigsaw piece?
5. I think (we're/where) going to play I Spy after lunch.

Looking at ... consonant blends *pl* and *sl*

Some consonants like to get together *without* a vowel between them. You can hear both their sounds blended together.
For example: the consonant ***l*** is often found with ***s*** as in ***sl****ip* and ***sl****ap* or with ***p*** as in ***pl****ay* and ***pl****ease*.

1. Underline examples of the consonant blend ***sl*** in this sentence:

   The slippery slime sent them sliding down the slope.

2. Underline examples of the consonant blend ***pl*** in this sentence:

   There are plenty of planes to play with at the playground.

Proofreading

Find six spelling mistakes and write the words correctly below. The first one has been done for you.

Its fun to go to the playground. If we take a bawl there are lots of games to playe. I pretend I'm king of the casle on the slipery dip. I also play hidee and tag with my friends.

1. It's
2. ______
3. ______
4. ______
5. ______
6. ______

Vocabulary power

Suffixes are letters added to the end of a word to change its meaning.
For example: play + ***ed*** = **played**.

Most words add suffixes without any changes but some words change their spelling.
For example: words that end with the letter ***e*** drop the ***e*** (***save*** → ***saved***).

Add the suffix ***ed*** to these words. The first one has been done for you.

1. bounce bounced
2. race ______
3. touch ______
4. save ______
5. kick ______
6. cheer ______

Read and learn

Read the text below. What do the words in **bold** mean?

Escargot (meaning *snail*) is a **French** game. Each person **hops** along the squares around a spiral shape. If you hop on a line, you **lose** a turn. If you don't, you **earn** a square for yourself. No-one can hop in 'your' square. You need a lot of **energy** to play this game!

Circle the answer closest in meaning to the word in **bold**. The first one has been done for you.

		a	b	c
1	**French**	different	friendly	(from France)
2	**hops**	moves forwards on one foot	circles	stays still
3	**lose**	have	miss	find
4	**earn**	take	save	get
5	**energy**	work	strength	skill

Puzzle

Can you guess what is meant from the way the letters are placed in each box?

1 CYCLE CYCLE CYCLE	2 R O ROADS D S
3 LE VEL	4 CIRGOINGCLES
5 T42	6 TRASTUCKFFIC

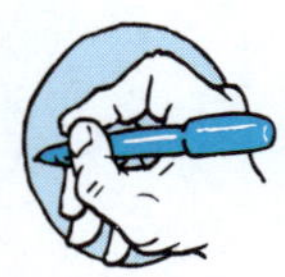

Your turn to write

Write down the steps you need to play a game of your choice (e.g. a card game, a board game or a playground game). At the end of your instructions, add a picture of the game being played.

Revise and edit your work. Check the spelling. Make a published copy for your teacher, parent or friend.

Tip!

Look at how instructions are written in **Reading for fun** below as a guide.

How to play ____________________

____

____

____

____

____

____

____

____

Reading for fun

1. Sit on a chair.
2. Lift your right foot from the ground.
3. Make clockwise circles with your right foot.
4. Draw the number six in the air with your right hand.
5. Your right foot will change direction as you draw in the air.
6. Can you trick your right foot? Try again … and again. Any luck?

☞ Answers on pages 109–110

7 Night and day

Quick fun

Put the words from the box in the order of shortest word to longest. The first one has been done for you.

sunlight	stars
moon	planet
rainbow	sky

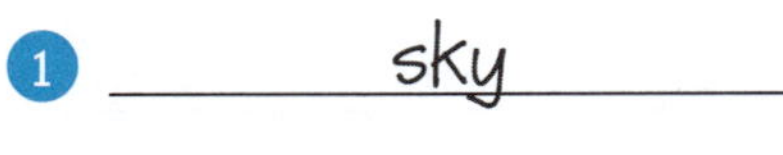

1. sky

2. __________
3. __________

4. __________
5. __________
6. __________

Topic spelling list

Use the **LOOK-SAY-COVER-WRITE-SAY-CHECK** strategy to learn these words.

cloudy	sunny	stars
sky	moon	planet
earth	spins	Saturn
telescope	sunlight	dark
moonlight	shadow	rainbow
daylight	tonight	today

Use this space to write out your topic words the first time. Use your own paper for extra practice.

Rewrite here those you had the most trouble with.

Spelling strategy

Word shapes

Thinking about the **shape** of a word can help you remember its spelling. Look at the pattern made by letters going above, below or on the line. For example: here is the word *sky*.

1 Fill in the boxes with the word *sunny*.

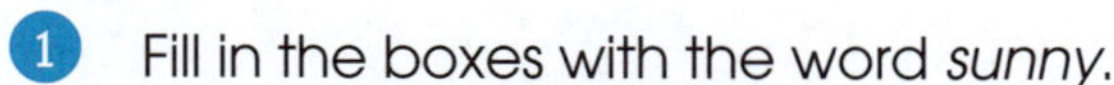

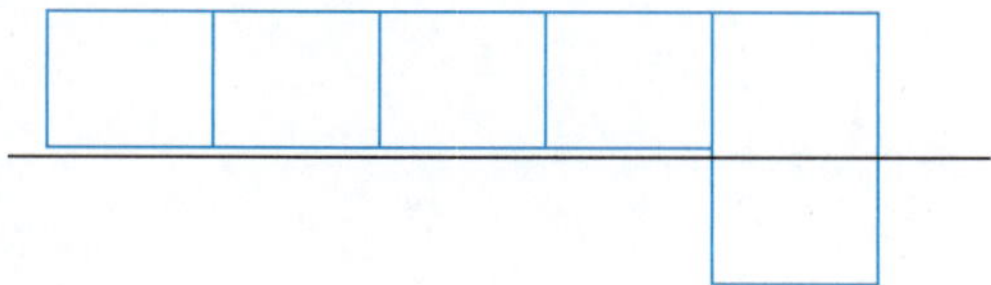

2 Fill in the boxes with the word *planet*.

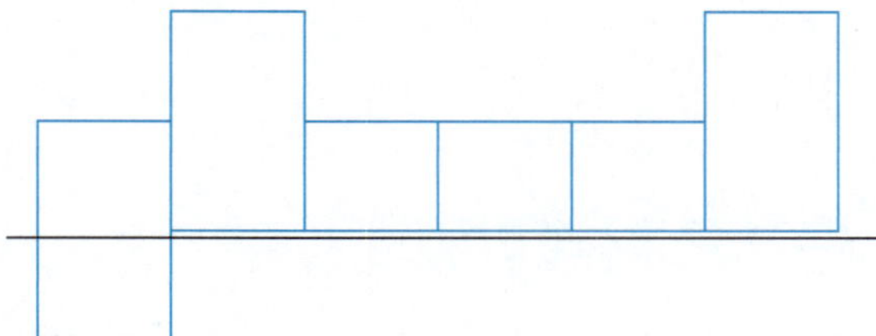

3 Fill in the boxes with the word *daylight*.

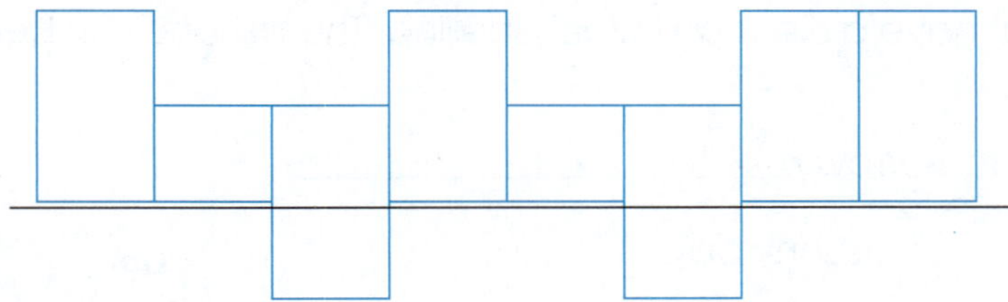

Fill in the gaps

Choose words from the **Topic spelling list** to complete these sentences. The first one has been done for you.

1 Today it is cool and cloudy__________.

2 Sometimes my s__________ is bigger than I am!

3 Earth is the third p__________ from the Sun.

4 The earth s__________ slowly all the time.

5 There is a full m__________ in the sky.

6 There will be fireworks t__________.

Tricky words

Many words are made by adding two words together. The new word is called a **compound word**. For example: ***moon*** + ***light*** makes ***moonlight***. It is easier to spell compound words when you break them into their parts.

Which two words are these compound words made from? The first one has been done for you.

1. starlight star + light
2. rainbow ____________
3. afternoon ____________
4. daylight ____________
5. spacecraft ____________
6. daytime ____________

Looking at…the letters *gh*

Sometimes when the letters **gh** are together in a word they stay silent.
For example: *si**gh**t, throu**gh***.

Fill in the spaces with words that have a silent **gh** in their spelling. The first one has been done for you.

1. We are having pancakes tomorrow n<u>ight</u>.
2. It is a b____________, sunny day.
3. Would you please turn on the l____________?
4. The spacecraft took f____________.
5. We m____________ get a new telescope.

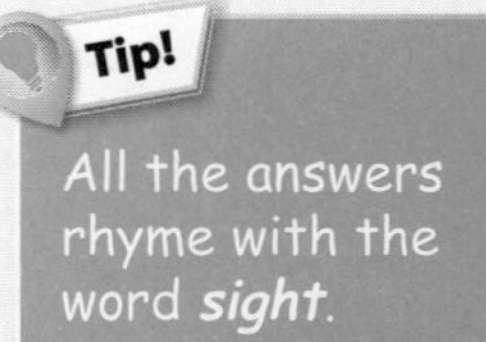

All the answers rhyme with the word ***sight***.

Proofreading

Find six spelling mistakes and write the words correctly below. The first one has been done for you.

My uncle has a telescop. Last nite the skye was cloudless. He said it was a good time to sea the moon. I also saw some starrs and a plannet. It was amazing!

1. telescope
2. ______
3. ______
4. ______
5. ______
6. ______

Vocabulary power

Nouns are naming words. Common nouns name people (e.g. *boy*), animals (e.g. *bat*), places (e.g. *sky*) and things (e.g. *rainbow*).

Label the people, animals, places and things in the picture with nouns from the box.

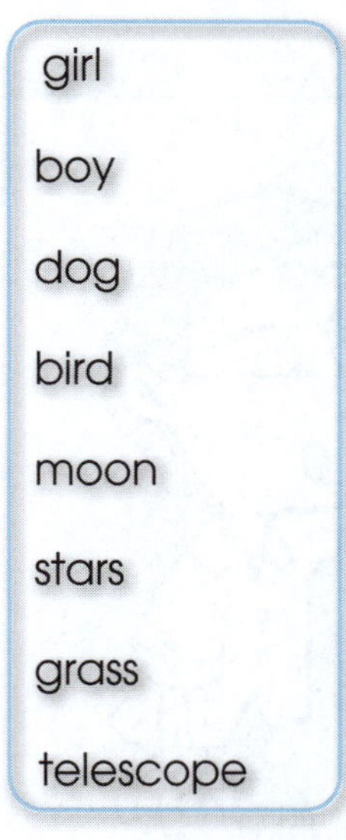

Read and learn

Read the text below. What do the words in **bold** mean?

Saturn is the second **largest** planet. It is big enough to **fit** more than 760 Earths! It **spins** faster than any planet **except** Jupiter. The rings **around** Saturn are mainly made of ice.

Circle the answer closest in meaning to the word in **bold**. The first one has been done for you.

1 **largest**	a tallest	b biggest (circled)	c smallest
2 **fit**	a hold	b carry	c wear
3 **spins** around	a jumps	b moves	c turns around and around
4 **except**	a accept	b other than	c with
5 **around**	a circling	b near	c over

Puzzle

Can you make at least six words of four or more letters from the word *telescope*? The first one has been done for you.

1 post
2 __________
3 __________
4 __________
5 __________
6 __________
7 __________
8 __________
9 __________
10 __________

Your turn to write

Write a story about a visitor from outer space. Give it a title. What does the visitor look like? What does he/she/it do? What does he/she/it say? What happens? At the end of your story, add a picture of the visitor from outer space.

Revise and edit your work. Check the spelling. Make a published copy for your teacher, parent or friend.

Title: ______________________________

____

____

____

____

____

____

____

____

____

____

Reading for fun

✦ **The more you have of me the less you see. What am I?**

❖ Darkness.

✦ **Why did the sun go to school?**

❖ To get brighter.

✦ **Why did the cow go to outer space?**

❖ To visit the Milky Way.

☞ Answers on page 110

8 From cover to cover

Quick fun

Draw a line from these labels to the picture of the book:

- cover
- cover picture
- spine
- title
- author's name.

Draw a line from these labels to the picture of the open book:

- chapter title
- page number.

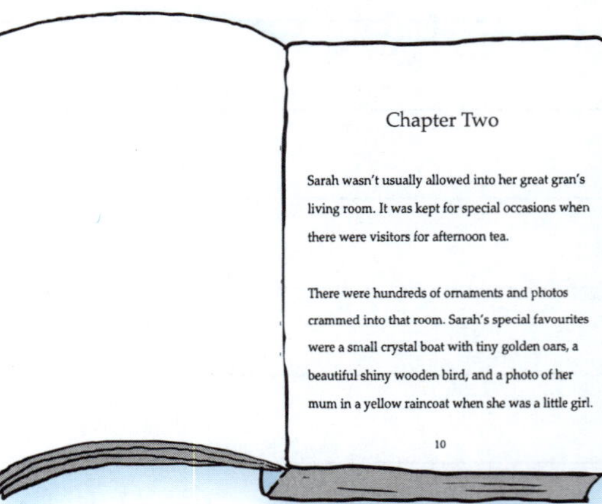

Chapter Two

Sarah wasn't usually allowed into her great gran's living room. It was kept for special occasions when there were visitors for afternoon tea.

There were hundreds of ornaments and photos crammed into that room. Sarah's special favourites were a small crystal boat with tiny golden oars, a beautiful shiny wooden bird, and a photo of her mum in a yellow raincoat when she was a little girl.

10

Topic spelling list

Use the **LOOK-SAY-COVER-WRITE-SAY-CHECK** strategy to learn these words.

book
cover
word
illustrator
index
information

page
title
chapter
library
story
picture

number
letter
author
shelves
fact
spine

Use this space to write out your topic words the first time. Use your own paper for extra practice.

Rewrite here those you had the most trouble with.

Spelling strategy

LOOK-SAY-COVER-WRITE-SAY-CHECK method

Choose six of the most challenging words from the **Topic Spelling list** and write them in Column 1 below. Then use the LOOK-SAY-COVER-WRITE-SAY-CHECK method to learn and practise their spellings.

1				
2				
3				
4				
5				
6				

Fill in the gaps

Choose words from the **Topic spelling list** to complete these sentences. The first one has been done for you.

1. I want to be an i llustrator when I grow up.
2. I like to choose my bedtime s_______________.
3. You can look that up in the i_______________.
4. Dr Seuss is my favourite a_______________.
5. That book is in the l_______________.
6. We found some i_______________ about planets.

Tricky words

The words ***there*** and ***their*** sound the same but have different meanings and spellings. Think of ways to remember the differences.
For example: ***there*** means in that place. It has the word ***here*** inside it. Think of the saying ***here*** and ***there*** to remind you.

Word	Meaning	Example
there	in that place	*I put the book over* ***there****.*
their	belonging to them	***Their*** *books are in* ***their*** *bags.*

Test your memory by writing the correct word (*there* or *their*) in these sentences without looking back at the different meanings.

1. They put (there/their) books away. ________________
2. He is over (there/their) reading King Kong. ________________
3. (There/Their) favourite story is Silly Billy. ________________
4. Are (there/their) any new books in the library? ________________

Looking at … *er* endings

The ***er*** sound at the end of a word can be spelt in different ways.
For example: *writ**er**, auth**or*** and *simil**ar***. There aren't any rules about which is the correct way, so it helps to know that ***er*** is used much more than the other spellings, and verbs ending in silent ***e*** mostly change to ***er*** (e.g. *make* → *mak**er***).

Who or what am I? The first one has been done for you.

Tip! These words all have ***er*** endings.

1. There are 26 of me in the alphabet. letter
2. I am something you use to count. ________________
3. I am on the front and the back of a book.

   ____
4. I teach children. ________________
5. I bake bread. ________________
6. I drive cars. ________________

Proofreading

Find six spelling mistakes and write the words correctly below. The first one has been done for you.

When I was small I loved a book caled *Where the Wild Things Are*.

Now I choose my own books from the libary. Yesterday I got out a book about repptiles. It wasn't a storey book. It had an indecks and lots of infomation.

1 called
2 ____________
3 ____________
4 ____________
5 ____________
6 ____________

Vocabulary power

Nouns are naming words. **Proper nouns** name particular people (e.g. *Cinderella*), animals (e.g. *Blinky Bill*), places (e.g. *Storyland*) and things (e.g. *Vegemite*). They always have capital letters.

Proper nouns can have more than one word in their name.
For example: *Treasure Island*.

Underline the proper nouns in these book titles. The first one has been done for you.

1 Goldilocks and the Three Bears
2 Jack and the Beanstalk
3 Hansel and Gretel
4 The Bunyip of Berkeley's Creek
5 King Kong
6 Alice in Wonderland
7 Tiddalik the Frog

Read and learn

Read the text below. What do the words in **bold** mean?

I looked up joeys in the **index** of a book about kangaroos. I **learned** they are **less** than 2 centimetres long when they are born. At first **joeys** are blind and bald. They **remain** in their mother's pouch and drink milk from her.

Circle the answer closest in meaning to the word in **bold**. The first one has been done for you.

	a	b	c
1 **index**	a a list of things (circled)	b spine	c pages
2 **learned**	a found out	b guessed	c heard
3 **less**	a more than	b about	c smaller than
4 **joeys**	a babies	b baby kangaroos	c boys called Joey
5 **remain**	a sit	b wait	c stay

Puzzle

The pictures below make a comic strip. But the artist has drawn his pictures in the wrong order! Number the pictures in the order they should be to tell a story.

Your turn to write

Write a story about something going wrong. Give it a title. What goes wrong? What happens next? At the end of your story, add a picture.

Revise and edit your work. Check the spelling. Make a published copy for your teacher, parent or friend.

Title: ______________________________

____

____

____

____

____

____

____

____

____

Reading for fun

Have you seen any of these books in the library?

Will He Win? by Bettie Wont

Don't Wake the Baby by Elsie Cries

A Bang on the Head by Esaw Starrs

Road Safety by Luke Bothways

The Haunted House by Hugo First

How to Make Money by Robin Banks

☞ Answers on pages 110–111

9 What's that building?

Quick fun

Find a word from the box that rhymes with each word below. The first one has been done for you.

church house wall tower school shops

What rhymes with:

1. mouse? house
2. cool? ____________
3. perch? ____________
4. cops? ____________
5. flower? ____________
6. call? ____________

Topic spelling list

Use the **LOOK-SAY-COVER-WRITE-SAY-CHECK** strategy to learn these words.

school	house	hospital
units	shops	offices
tower	museum	gallery
palace	pyramid	castle
barn	church	temple
wall	roof	stairs

Use this space to write out your topic words the first time. Use your own paper for extra practice.

Rewrite here those you had the most trouble with.

Spelling strategy

Word shapes

Thinking about the **shape** of a word can help you remember its spelling. Look at the pattern made by letters going above, below or on the line. For example, here is the word *shops*:

1. Fill in the boxes with the word *school*.

2. Fill in the boxes with the word *temple*.

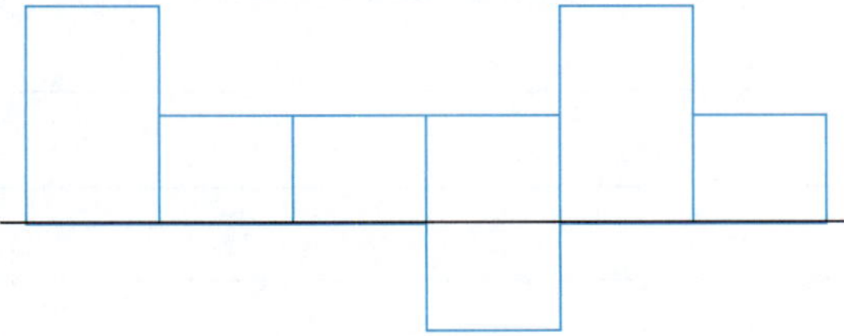

3. Fill in the boxes with the word *pyramid*.

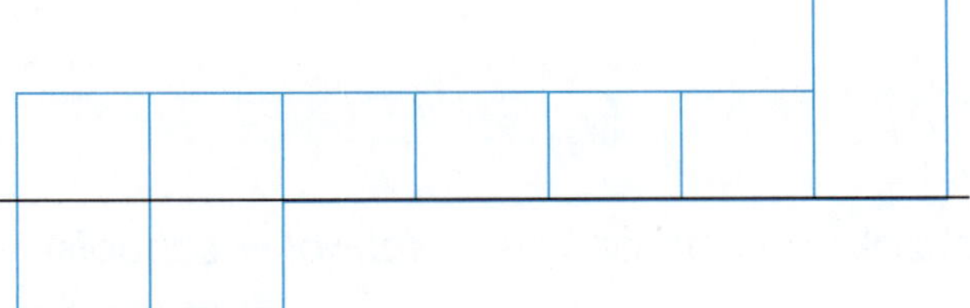

Fill in the gaps

Choose words from the **Topic spelling list** to complete these sentences. The first one has been done for you.

1. I climbed a hundred s<u>tairs</u>____________.
2. The ambulance took her to h__________________.
3. We saw some dinosaur bones at the m__________________.
4. I'm the king of the c__________________.
5. I have posters up on the w__________________ in my bedroom.
6. Mum and Dad go to their o__________________ in the city.

Tricky words

Some words with three letters sound like the name of a single letter.
For example: ***are*** (**R**), ***you*** (**U**) and ***see*** (**C**).
Making up a funny saying that uses the three letters in each word can help you remember their spelling.

You could use these ideas or make up your own.

*are—**a**re **r**obot's **e**ars*

*you—**y**ou **o**r **u**ncle*

*see—**s**ee **e**very **e**gg*

Repeat your saying each time you write these words. Practise by writing these sentences.

1. The shops are near the church. ______________________
____
2. Did you go to the station? ______________________
____
3. Can I see inside the palace? ______________________
____

Looking at … plurals *s, ss* and *ies*

In order to make most singular words plural, you add an **s** (e.g. ***school*** → ***schools***).

For some words, such as those ending in **s** or **ss**, add **es** (e.g. ***gas*** → ***gases***; ***glass*** → ***glasses***).

For some words that end in a consonant followed by a **y**, add **ies** (e.g. ***gallery*** → ***galleries***).

Make these words plural. The first one has been done for you.

1 yes	yeses	5 princess	______
2 bus	______	6 city	______
3 kiss	______	7 class	______
4 baby	______	8 country	______

Proofreading

Find six spelling mistakes and write the words correctly below. The first one has been done for you.

We took a lift to the top of the art galery. From the rouf I could see a cherch with a very high touwer and a hospittal. Then we went down the stares to see the paintings.

1.  gallery
2.  ________________
3. ________________
4. ________________
5. ________________
6. ________________

Vocabulary power

Adjectives are describing words. They give information about nouns such as their size, shape, colour, number, and so on.
For example: in the sentence *The **tall**, **green** building is over there,* the adjectives ***tall*** and ***green*** describe the building.

Circle the adjectives that describe the underlined nouns in these sentences.
The first one has been done for you.

1. The (old) barn is near the shed.
2. Have you noticed the round tower?
3. There are two churches in our village.
4. I saw some interesting, old bones in the museum.
5. We have red tiles on our roof.
6. Have you seen our new house?

Read and learn

Read the text below. What do the words in **bold** mean?

Pyramids were **built** in Egypt a long time ago. When kings or queens died, they were buried in a **tomb**. It was **placed** in the pyramid with lots of treasure. Some pyramids had **secret** passages. I **suppose** they were made to stop thieves from finding the treasure.

Circle the answer closest in meaning to the word in **bold**. The first one has been done for you.

1. **built** — a made (circled) — b planned — c thought of
2. **tomb** — a tower — b burial place — c house
3. **placed** — a held — b made — c put
4. **secret** — a hidden — b quiet — c tiny
5. **suppose** — a accept — b think — c dream

Puzzle

Complete the puzzle with words from the Topic spelling list.

ACROSS

1. building you stay in when you are sick
3. building where things are displayed
4. building where a prince or princess lives
5. building with blocks of flats

DOWN

1. buildings that people live in
2. buildings of kings

Your turn to write

Imagine you are someone who lives in either a palace or a lighthouse. Write about a day in your life. Choose a date. Who are you? What happens? What do you do?

Revise and edit your work. Check the spelling. Make a published copy for your teacher, parent or friend.

Date: ______________________

Reading for fun

✦ **What did one wall say to the other?**

❖ Meet you at the corner.

✦ **If the red house was made out of red bricks, and the blue house was made out of blue bricks, what was the greenhouse made out of?**

❖ Glass.

✦ **What do you get when a chicken lays an egg on top of a barn?**

❖ An egg roll.

☞ Answers on page 111

10 How does it feel?

Quick fun

Unscramble the letters to make the words in the box. The first one has been done for you.

sharp
hard
smooth
rough
dry
sticky

1. ogrhu ___rough___
2. rdah ____________
3. ckitsy ____________
4. ryd ____________
5. pshra ____________
6. tsoomh ____________

Topic spelling list

Use the **LOOK-SAY-COVER-WRITE-SAY-CHECK** strategy to learn these words.

cold	damp	dry
furry	hairy	hot
lumpy	rough	sharp
slimy	smooth	prickly
sticky	velvety	wet
scratchy	soft	hard

Use this space to write out your topic words the first time. Use your own paper for extra practice.

Rewrite here those you had the most trouble with.

Spelling strategy

Breaking words into syllables

Remember that a **syllable** is a unit of sound within a word. One syllable makes one beat. You can clap the beats to find how many there are in a word.
For example:
The words ***cold*** and ***dry*** get one clap each. They are one syllable words.
The words ***furry*** and ***hairy*** get two claps each. They are two syllable words.
Three claps make three syllables, and so on.

How many syllables does each word have? The first one has been done for you.

	Word	How many syllables?
1	damp	one
2	hot	
3	lumpy	
4	rough	
5	slimy	
6	smooth	
7	velvety	

Fill in the gaps

Choose words from the **Topic spelling list** to complete these sentences. The first one has been done for you.

1. That knife is very sharp.
2. Her dressing gown is soft and v________________.
3. This ice block has made my mouth s________________.
4. The rain has made my hair w________________.
5. The princess said the pea made her mattress l________________!
6. The gorilla's head is h________________.

Tricky words

Apostrophes (') are used to show where letters have been left out. This means that the word ***it's***, spelt with an apostrophe, is short for ***it is***.

The words ***it's*** and ***its*** sound the same but have different meanings and spellings. Think of what the apostrophe means to remember their differences.

Word	Meaning	Example
it's	it is	***It's*** *raining today.*
its	belonging to it	*Is this his, hers or* ***its****?*

Underline the correct spelling of the word (*it's* or *its*) in these sentences.

1. It's/Its much cooler over there.
2. The stamp has lost it's/its sticky side.
3. I don't know why it's/its so slippery here.
4. That bird can't find it's/its worm.

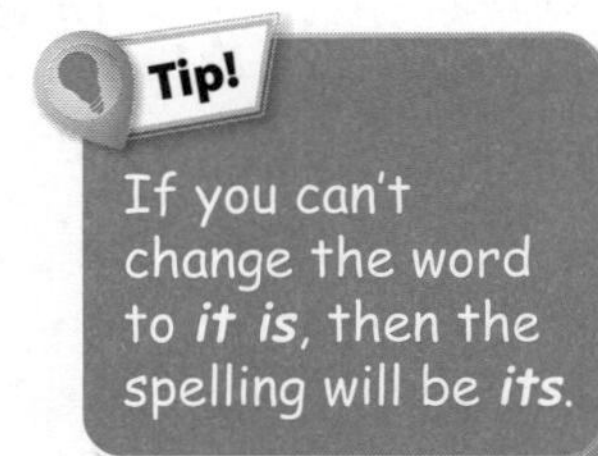

Looking at ... consonant digraphs *th*, *ch* and *sh*

When some consonants are side by side they make a single sound.
For example: ***th*** as in ***th****is*, ***th****at* or ***th****e o****th****er*, ***ch*** as in ***Ch****itty, **Ch**itty Bang Bang*, ***sh*** as in ***Sh****e sells sea **sh**ells on the sea **sh**ore.*

Underline the consonant pair ***th*** in these sentences. The first one has been done for you.

1. That feels thin and smooth.
2. I cut my thumb on the thick thorn.
3. They thought the bath water was too hot.

Underline the consonant pair ***ch*** in these sentences.

4. Chicken pox is very itchy.
5. There is a patch of sticky chewing gum on this bench.

Underline the consonant pair ***sh*** in these sentences.

6. That sharp sword makes me shiver and shake.
7. She polished her shiny shoes with a soft brush.

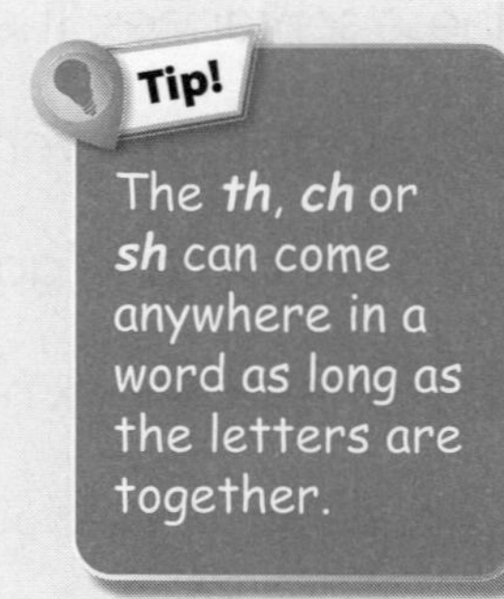

Proofreading

Find six spelling mistakes and write the words correctly below. The first one has been done for you.

My baby brother has lots of softe toys. He has a hairye dog, a velvity rabbit and some fury teddy bears. Its easy to see his favourite teddy. The fur on it's back is all worn off.

1. soft
2. ______
3. ______
4. ______
5. ______
6. ______

Vocabulary power

When you use an adjective to compare two things, you add the suffix ***er***, as in, ***cold*** → ***colder***. For example: Today is a *colder* day than yesterday.

Many words add ***er*** without any changes but some words change their spelling. For example: words that end with the letter ***e*** drop the ***e*** (***late*** → ***later***) and one syllable words that end in a consonant, double the consonant (***fat*** → ***fatter***).

Some words completely change. For example: ***good*** → ***better***, ***bad*** → ***worse***.

How would you change these words to compare two things? The first one has been done for you.

1. long → longer
2. hot → ______
3. smooth → ______
4. soft → ______
5. bad → ______
6. wet → ______

Read and learn

Read the text below. What do the words in **bold** mean?

> Last night, I **dreamt** about a **friendly** dragon. It had **rows** of spiky scales on its tail. They looked too **prickly** to touch. I patted the **sleek** skin on its back instead.

Circle the answer closest in meaning to the word in **bold**. The first one has been done for you.

1 **dreamt**	a thought when asleep	b thought	c saw
2 **friendly**	a wicked	b kindly	c evil
3 **rows**	a circles	b lines of	c dots
4 **prickly**	a soft	b upright	c with sharp points
5 **sleek**	a very smooth	b hot	c cool

Puzzle

What is in the socks?

You need six socks and six objects to put in the socks. You could use an eraser, a coin, a golf ball, a stone, a bath plug, screwed-up foil, a plastic toy, a cake of soap, and so on.

Ask a parent or friend to close their eyes and guess what is in each sock by feeling the outside. They can only have one guess. Give them a score out of six. Let them try to guess any they got wrong by feeling inside the sock.

Then ask someone to give you a turn.

Your turn to write

Draw a fierce monster with the following features:

- scaly skin
- sharp claws
- pointy teeth
- hairy legs
- whirring wings
- smoking nostrils.

Add labels for these parts to your drawing.

Revise and edit your work. Check the spelling. Make a published copy for your teacher, parent or friend.

Reading for fun

✦ What did one pig say to another at the beach?
❖ I'm bacon.

✦ How does a frog feel when he has a broken leg?
❖ Unhoppy.

✦ What do you call a grizzly bear caught in the rain?
❖ A drizzly bear.

 ☞ Answers on page 111

Review 2

Now let's see what you remember of the words you learnt in Units 6–10. There are six tests in this review. You could do them all in one session, or you could break them up and do them over a few days.

Step 1 Look at each group of words in the test to revise the spellings.

Step 2 Cover the five words up and test yourself (column 2). Try to do all five words in one go.

Step 3 Write your score out of 5 in the box. If you got any words wrong, go back and study them again.

Step 4 If possible, ask someone to test you on the words later—an hour or even a day later (column 3).

Test 1

Study	Test yourself	Test with another person
swing slippery skipping running puzzle	/5	/5
football cricket rounders hopscotch chess	/5	/5
moon cloudy sunny telescope dark	/5	/5
	Total score = out of 15	Total score = out of 15

Test 2

Study	Test yourself	Test with another person
shadow rainbow tonight today earth	/5	/5
book page cover title word	/5	/5
writer author story information picture	/5	/5
school tower museum church palace	/5	/5
	Total score = out of 20	Total score = out of 20

Test 3

Study	Test yourself	Test with another person
wall roofs stairs barn hospital	/5	/5
furry hairy slimy lumpy smooth	/5	/5
velvety sticky soft hard prickly	/5	/5
are you where there place	/5	/5
	Total score = out of 20	Total score = out of 20

Test 4

Write the **bold** words correctly. An example has been done for you. Count your score when you have finished the test.

Spelling mistakes	Correct words	Score ✓ ✗
Where going to Luna Park.	We're	
1 Are you going **their** after school?		
2 **Its** a sunny day today.		
3 Did you **sea** the snake?		
4 We have a new **teachor**.		
5 The **busses** have arrived.		
	Total score	/ 5

Test 5

How many **syllables** do these words have? An example has been done for you. Count your score when you have finished the test.

Word	Number of syllables	Score ✓ ✗
library	three	
1 church		
2 telescope		
3 building		
4 night		
5 sunny		
	Total	/ 5

Test 6

Match the words in Column 1 with their opposites in Column 2. An example has been done for you.

Column 1	Column 2	Score ✓ ✗
hot	cold	
1 warm	cloudy	
2 rough	dry	
3 sunny	light	
4 wet	smooth	
5 dark	cool	
	Total	/ 5

Grand total	
Test 1	
Test 2	
Test 3	
Test 4	
Test 5	
Test 6	
Total	/ 70

☞ Answers on pages 111–112

11 Now and then

Quick fun

Put these words in the order in which they take place. The first one has been done for you.

last second third first

1 first

2 ______

3 ______

4 ______

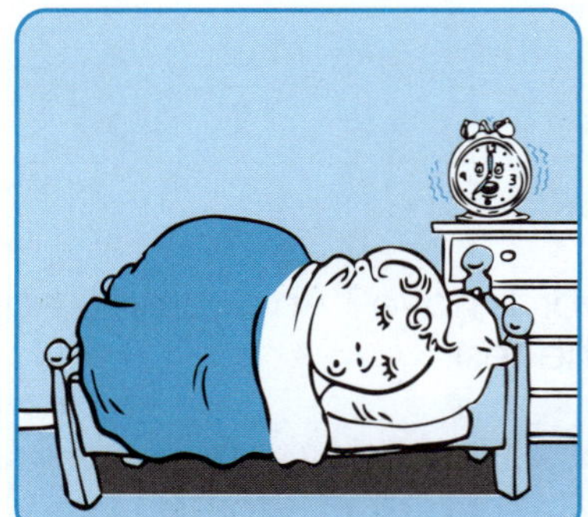

tomorrow

yesterday

today

5 ______

6 ______

7 ______

Topic spelling list

Use the **LOOK-SAY-COVER-WRITE-SAY-CHECK** strategy to learn these words.

after	before	next
soon	almost	often
late	early	first
second	third	last
finally	nearly	tomorrow
yesterday	when	while

Use this space to write out your topic words the first time. Use your own paper for extra practice.

Rewrite here those you had the most trouble with.

Spelling strategy

Little words in big words

Some words have other words hidden inside them.
For example: ***early*** has the word ***ear*** inside it. This can help you remember its spelling.

Find a word hidden inside these words. The first one has been done for you.

1. yesterday ______yes, day______
2. last ____________________
3. often ____________________
4. late ____________________
5. before ____________________
6. finally ____________________

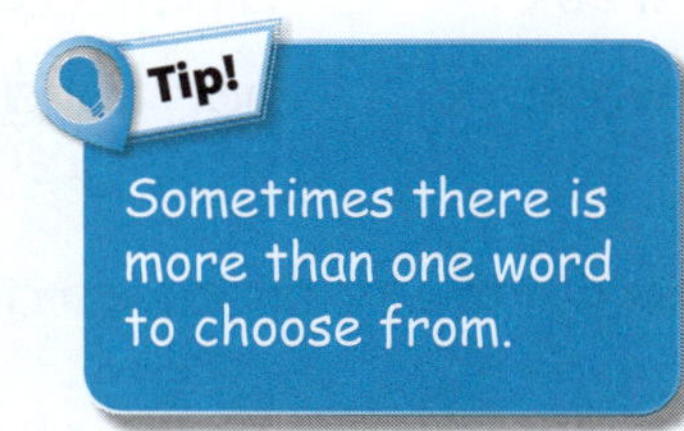

Fill in the gaps

Choose words from the **Topic spelling list** to complete these sentences. The first one has been done for you.

1. While ____________________ you slept, I fed the dog.
2. My birthday is n____________________ week.
3. We ate our vegetables b____________________ our dessert.
4. W____________________ are we leaving here?
5. Have you f____________________ mended my go-cart?
6. Our cricket match begins s____________________.

Tricky words

The words **week** and **weak** sound the same but have different meanings and spellings. Think of a way to remember the difference.
For example: the words ***weak tea*** are both spelt with the letters ***ea***.

Word	Meaning	Example
week	a period of seven days	*Next **week** we go on holiday.*
weak	not strong	*Mum likes her tea **weak**.*

Cross out the incorrect word (*week* or *weak*) in these sentences.

1. (Week/Weak) is the opposite of strong.
2. I have a (week/weak) muscle in my leg.
3. The camping trip lasts a (week/weak).
4. School starts the (week/weak) after next.

Looking at…trigraphs *tch* and *igh*

A trigraph is a single sound made by three letters side by side. Some trigraphs form a single word (e.g. ***ewe, owe***). Some are made by consonants (e.g. *ca**tch***). Others are made by a combination of consonants and vowels (e.g. *s**igh***).

Complete these sentences with a word that includes a trigraph. Circle the trigraph within your word. The first one has been done for you.

1. Last ___night___ I had a scary dream!
2. Our first football ________________ is next Monday after school.
3. I spy with my little ________________ a photo of my dog.
4. My ________________ to Perth was in an airbus.
5. Mum told me not to ________________ my itch.

Proofreading

Find six spelling mistakes and write the words correctly below. The first one has been done for you.

"Are we neerly there yet, Dad?"

"We'll be there sune, son."

"The game is allmost starting."

"Sorry. We're runing late this weak."

"It's ok, Dad. We can be erly next time."

1. nearly
2. __________
3. __________
4. __________
5. __________
6. __________

Vocabulary power

Remember that an **antonym** is a word opposite in meaning to another word.
For example: ***late*** is the opposite of ***early***.

Choose an antonym from the box to replace the underlined words. The first one has been done for you.

now after never last later

1. Dad had the <u>first</u> dance with Mum. last
2. I <u>always</u> go to bed at 7 o'clock. __________
3. I'll be ready <u>soon</u>. __________
4. Give that to me <u>later</u>, please. __________
5. We ate our salad <u>before</u> our soup. __________

Read and learn

Read the text below. What do the words in **bold** mean?

The **first** thing to do is **crack** two eggs into a bowl. Then you pour in a little milk. **Next** you get a fork and **blend** the mixture. After that pour the mixture into a non-stick pan. Cook for just a **few** minutes. You have made an omelette!

Circle the answer closest in meaning to the word in **bold**. The first one has been done for you.

1 **first**	a only	b main	c before anything else
2 **crack**	a break	b smash	c throw
3 **Next**	a before	b later	c straight after
4 **blend**	a mix together	b whizz	c beat
5 **few**	a many	b not many	c lots of

Puzzle

Jimmy and his friend, Jake, use a secret code. Here it is.

A	B	C	D	E	F	G	H	I	J	K	K	M
1	2	3	4	5	6	7	8	9	10	11	12	13
N	O	P	Q	R	S	T	U	V	W	X	Y	Z
14	15	16	17	18	19	20	21	22	23	24	25	26

Can you decode the message Jimmy wrote to Jake?

8/9 10/1/11/5

____

9 3/1/14/20 13/5/5/20 25/15/21 14/15/23. 9 3/1/14 13/5/5/20 25/15/21

____

20/15/13/15/18/18/15/23 1/20 15/21/18 3/21/2/2/25. 19/5/5/

____

25/15/21 20/8/5/14.

____

10/9/13/13/25

____

Your turn to write

Fill in this calendar with things you want to do over the next week. Add a symbol (e.g. a smiley mouth, a heart or a thumbs up) to mark the things you most look forward to doing.

Day	Date	Things I want to do
Monday		
Tuesday		
Wednesday		
Thursday		
Friday		
Saturday		
Sunday		

Revise and edit your work. Check the spelling. Make a published copy for your teacher, parent or friend.

Reading for fun

Words that sound the same but have different meanings are often used in making jokes. These are called **puns**. When you 'get' the pun, you get the joke!

Can you find the pun in each of these jokes? The first one has been done for you.

1 Why was everyone so tired on April 1st?
They had just finished a March of 31 days.
The pun in this joke is March/march.

2 Why are Saturday and Sunday the strongest days?
Because all the others are week-days.
The pun in this joke is:

____

3 What does a clock do when it's hungry?
Goes back for seconds!
The puns in this joke are:

____

☞ Answers on page 112

12 Likes and dislikes

Quick fun

Write the words from the box in alphabetical order. The first one has been done for you.

worse	like
love	dislike
bad	awful

1 awful

2

3

4

5

6

Use this space to write out your topic words the first time. Use your own paper for extra practice.

Topic spelling list

Use the **LOOK-SAY-COVER-WRITE-SAY-CHECK** strategy to learn these words.

love	hate	like
dislike	prefer	want
very	good	better
best	least	bad
worse	worst	yummy
yucky	awful	favourite

Rewrite here those you had the most trouble with.

Spelling strategy

LOOK-SAY-COVER-WRITE-SAY-CHECK method

Choose six of the most challenging words from the **Topic Spelling list** and write them in Column 1 below. Then use the LOOK-SAY-COVER-WRITE-SAY-CHECK method to learn and practise their spellings.

1				
2				
3				
4				
5				
6				

Fill in the gaps

Choose words from the **Topic spelling list** to complete these sentences. The first one has been done for you.

1. I dislike____________ peanut butter.
2. Mum thinks yoghurt is y____________ but I think it's y____________.
3. Sarah is my b____________ friend.
4. We all w____________ to go to Luna Park.
5. I p____________ watching TV to ice skating.
6. Your painting is b____________ than mine.

Tricky words

Some words are spelt and sound the same, but have different meanings. Find the word from the box that has these different meanings.

like	bank
trip	fair

1. **a** stumble
   b a journey

   The word is: ______________________

2. **a** land beside a river
   b a place where money is kept

   The word is: ______________________

3. **a** pale in colour
   b a market with stalls and entertainments

   The word is: ______________________

4. **a** similar to something else
   b be fond of

   The word is:

Looking at … words ending in *y*

Words that end with a long ***i*** sound (as in *my*) or a long ***e*** sound (as in *very*) are nearly always spelt with a ***y***.

List five words rhyming with *my* that end with a long ***i*** sound spelt with ***y***. The first one has been done for you.

1. ________cry________
2. ______________________
3. ______________________
4. ______________________
5. ______________________

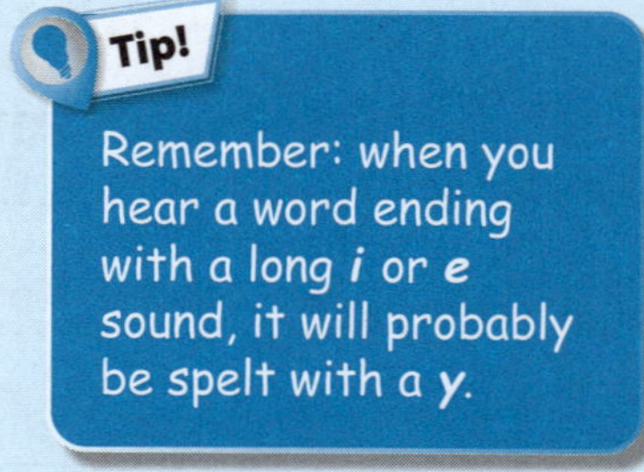

List three words from the **Topic spelling list** that end with a long ***e*** sound spelt with ***y***.

6. ______________________
7. ______________________
8. ______________________

Proofreading

Find six spelling mistakes and write the words correctly below. The first one has been done for you.

We are going out for diner. I hop I can have noodles. My sister preffers pizza. My brother always loikes to have pasta. Mum and Dad have a verie hard time choosing their favourit dish.

1. dinner
2. 
3. 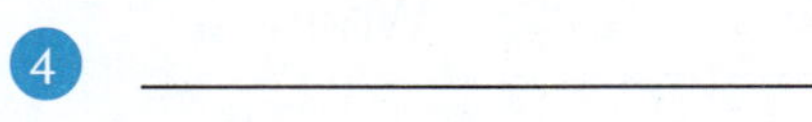
4. 
5. 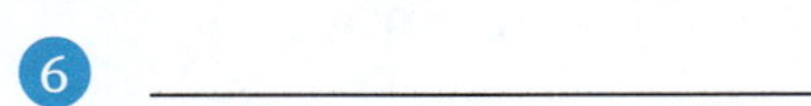
6. ____________

Vocabulary power

When you use an adjective to compare more than two things, you add the suffix ***est*** to the word (***bright*** → ***brightest***).
For example: That is the ***brightest*** star in the sky.

Many words add ***est*** without any changes but some words change their spelling.
For example: for words that end with the letter ***e*** drop the ***e*** (***late*** → ***latest***), for one-syllable words that end in a consonant double the consonant (***fat*** → ***fattest***).
Some words completely change.
For example: ***good*** → ***best***, ***bad*** → ***worst***.

Change the adjective in brackets to complete each sentence correctly. The first one has been done for you.

1. She is the (kind) kindest girl in her class.
2. That is the (unkind) ____________ thing anyone could do.
3. This is the (ripe) ____________ peach in the dish.
4. I have the (sweet) ____________ tooth in our family.
5. It is the (cold) ____________ day of winter.
6. I have the (bad) ____________ cold I have ever had.

Read and learn

Read the text below. What do the words in **bold** mean?

We can't **decide** what to give my sister for her birthday. **Perhaps** she'd like ice skates because she goes skating **often**. She **might** like a scooter. I'm **certain** she'd love a digital watch. That is the best choice.

Circle the answer closest in meaning to the word in **bold**. The first one has been done for you.

1. **decide** a know (b make up our mind) c tell
2. **Perhaps** a Then b Maybe c When
3. **often** a sometimes b once c many times
4. **might** a will b shall c may
5. **certain** a sure b thinking c knowing

Puzzle

Find these words in the word search puzzle below. Words go across and down.

love like hate want prefer need choose

y	s	n	g	r	j	x	y	c	h
p	s	h	l	c	y	i	u	n	o
m	g	k	i	h	k	k	w	l	n
e	g	p	k	o	r	l	o	v	e
f	m	l	e	o	k	h	a	l	e
a	b	e	q	s	m	i	e	k	d
w	h	a	t	e	n	f	i	q	d
w	a	n	t	h	n	k	p	w	s
p	r	e	f	e	r	f	n	s	p
l	m	q	n	t	v	u	z	b	k

Your turn to write

Write about what you like and dislike most.

The foods I like best are:

1 ______________________

2 ______________________

The foods I like least are:

1 ______________________

2 ______________________

The games I like best are:

1 ______________________

2 ______________________

The games I like least are:

1 ______________________

2 ______________________

Now you choose a topic.

The ______________ I like best are:

1 ______________________

2 ______________________

The ______________ I like least are:

1 ______________________

2 ______________________

Revise and edit your work. Check the spelling. Make a published copy for your teacher, parent or friend.

Reading for fun

Which riddle do you like best out of these below?

Answer: I like riddle number __________ best.

1 What do you call a dinosaur with no eyes?
Do-you-think-he-saw-us.

2 Why is 6 afraid of 7?
Because 7, 8, 9.

3 What do you call a man with four planks on his head?
I don't know. But Edward Woodward would.

Answers on page 112

13 Doing things

Quick fun

Put the words from the box into alphabetical order. The first one has been done for you.

driving	making
flying	building
helping	drawing

1. building
2. ______
3. ______
4. ______
5. ______
6. ______

Use this space to write out your topic words the first time. Use your own paper for extra practice.

Topic spelling list

Use the **LOOK-SAY-COVER-WRITE-SAY-CHECK** strategy to learn these words.

digging	planting	gardening
selling	mending	drawing
driving	helping	singing
writing	making	cooking
camping	flying	building
cycling	recycling	canoeing

Rewrite here those you had the most trouble with.

Spelling strategy

Learn a spelling rule: hard and soft *c*

The letter ***c*** can make a hard sound as in ***cat***, or a soft sound as in ***city***. The spelling rule is that ***c*** always makes a hard sound unless it is followed by the letters ***e***, ***i*** or ***y***. This is why ***kitten***, for example, is spelt with a ***k*** and not a ***c***. If it had a ***c*** it would be said as ***sitten***!

Does the underlined ***c*** in these words make a soft or a hard sound? The first one has been done for you.

1. cycling soft
2. canoeing ______________
3. camping ______________
4. circling ______________
5. cooking ______________
6. recycling ______________

Fill in the gaps

Choose words from the **Topic spelling list** to complete these sentences. The first one has been done for you.

1. Are you planting carrots there?
2. Mum is d______________ a new garden bed.
3. I like w______________ our shopping lists.
4. What is your baby brother b______________ with those bricks?
5. We are s______________ raffle tickets at our sausage sizzle.
6. I went c______________ on the river.

Tricky words

The words ***hour*** and ***our*** sound the same but have different meanings and spellings. Think of a way to remember the difference:
For example: an ***hour*** passes silently and there is a silent ***h*** in its spelling.

Word	Meaning	Example
hour	sixty minutes of time	*It took us an **hour** to drive there.*
our	belonging to us	*We took **our** canoe to camp.*

Cross out the incorrect word (*hour* or *our*) in the text below.

(Hour/Our) class wants everyone at (hour/our) school to recycle drink cans.

We spent the lunch (hour/our) planning how to make this happen.

A group of us stayed after school for an (hour/our) to work on the plan.

Looking at ... doubling consonants

If a word has one syllable, one short vowel and one consonant at the end, you double the final consonant when you add a vowel suffix (e.g. ***ing***).
For example: shop + ***ing*** becomes **shopping**.

Add the suffix ***ing*** to these words. The first one has been done for you.

1. dig digging
2. hop ____________
3. cook ____________
4. get ____________
5. knit ____________
6. garden ____________

Proofreading

Find six spelling mistakes and write the words correctly below. The first one has been done for you.

It is fun to go campping and to canoe on the river. I love cicling on my new bike.

I like gardenning sometimes but not for more than an our. I really like flying

papper planes. What do you like doeing best?

1. camping
2. ________________
3. ________________
4. ________________
5. ________________
6. ________________

Vocabulary power

Adverbs are words that can add meaning to verbs. Writers use them to tell how things happen. For example: in the sentence *She wrote her answers carefully,* the adverb ***carefully*** tells how she ***wrote***.

Circle the adverbs that add meaning to the underlined verbs. The first one has been done for you.

1. He sang the song (loudly.)
2. He rode his skateboard cleverly.
3. We flew slowly towards the airport.
4. He played his trumpet noisily.
5. I quickly drew a picture of her.
6. I stood still while she took my photo.

Read and learn

Read the text below. What do the words in **bold** mean?

> In our family, everyone **except** me has a hobby.
> Mum is **building** a birdhouse. Dad is **training** for a
> high jump competition. My brother **keeps** stamps.
> I like being **outdoors** best. Maybe I'll collect rocks.

Circle the answer closest in meaning to the word in **bold**. The first one has been done for you.

1 **except**	a and	b but (circled)	c even
2 **building**	a drawing	b breaking	c making
3 **training**	a going	b practising	c doing
4 **keeps**	a uses	b does	c saves
5 **outdoors**	a there	b outside	c here

Puzzle

Can you make at least seven words of four or more letters from the word *gardening*?
The first one has been done for you.

1. read
2. ______
3. ______
4. ______
5. ______
6. ______
7. ______
8. ______

Your turn to write

Write about a hobby you have or a hobby you would like to take up. Describe what you do and what makes your hobby worth doing. Add a picture of the things you need to do your hobby.

Revise and edit your work. Check the spelling. Make a published copy for your teacher, parent or friend.

Title: ______________________________

____

____

____

____

____

____

____

Reading for fun

✦ **Why didn't the dog want to play football?**
Because he was a boxer.

✦ **What insect doesn't play well in goal?**
A fumble bee.

✦ **What was the carpet's favourite sport?**
Rugby.

☞ Answers on pages 112–113

14 Tech talk

Quick fun

Unscramble the letters to make the words in the box. The first one has been done for you.

website
computer
telephone
email
mouse
screen

1. meali ______email______
2. sbwetei ____________
3. cneres ____________
4. leteonhpe ____________
5. smueo ____________
6. tupmocre ____________

Topic spelling list

Use the **LOOK-SAY-COVER-WRITE-SAY-CHECK** strategy to learn these words.

computer	mouse	mobile
telephone	television	screen
website	internet	save
print	email	press
font	icon	image
text	search	online

Use this space to write out your topic words the first time. Use your own paper for extra practice.

Rewrite here those you had the most trouble with.

Spelling strategy

Memory tricks

You can remember how to spell a hard word with a memory trick like the following.

1. Make up a funny sentence.
   For example: ***P**urple **h**air **o**n **n**oisy **e**mus* could remind you how to spell the tricky word ***phone***.
2. Put words together that repeat a spelling pattern.
   For example: *There's a m**ou**se in the h**ou**se* could remind you of the ***ou*** spelling pattern.
3. Think of your own trick. The word *image* is difficult to spell. How could you remember its spelling?

Fill in the gaps

Choose words from the **Topic spelling list** to complete these sentences. The first one has been done for you.

1. What is your favourite program on television.
2. I found that information on the i________________.
3. Click this i________________ on the screen to read a story.
4. Mum rang Dad at the shops from her m________________.
5. Our school has its own w________________.
6. I sent an e________________ to my friend in India.

Tricky words

Some words are spelt and sound the same, but have different meanings. Find the words from the **Topic spelling list** that have these different meanings.

1. **a** a net of thin wire that goes over a window to keep out insects
   b a thin wall used to separate things
   c the smooth glass part of a computer or television

   The word is: ____________________

2. **a** write in letters that aren't joined together
   b publish with the help of a machine
   c text in a book or on a screen

   The word is: ____________________

3. Can you think of two different meanings for the word *mouse*?

   ____

   ____

4. Can you think of three different meanings for the word *mobile*?

   ____

   ____

   ____

Looking at … words ending with *sion*

The *shun* sound at the end of words is spelt in different ways. One common spelling is ***sion*** as in ***television***. Words that end in ***sion*** often name nouns that are things or ideas.

Choose a word from the box to put in the sentences below.
The first one has been done for you.

explosion	discussion	decision	revision	permission

1. The teacher said I had ___permission___ to go online.
2. There was a big ____________________ when the television blew up.
3. We had a ____________________ in class today about ads on television.
4. Have you made a ____________________ about which website is the best?
5. We are doing ____________________ for our test.

Proofreading

Find six spelling mistakes and write the words correctly below. The first one has been done for you.

We have a computter at home. Mum lets me use it to serch for information. I am doing a project on the telefone. I laughed when I fowned Mr Bell was the name of it's inventor. I safed a picture of him.

1. computer
2. ______
3. ______
4. ______
5. ______
6. ______

Vocabulary power

Prefixes are letters added to the beginning of a word. Knowing what a prefix means can help with spelling and understanding words.
For example: the prefix ***tele*** means *from far away*.

The word ***television*** is made up of the prefix ***tele*** + ***vision***. A ***television*** is a machine you watch. It shows pictures and sounds sent from far away.

Tip! The answers begin with the prefix ***tele***.

What am I?

1. something that lets you talk to people who are far away ______
2. something you look through to see things far away ______
3. a toy from an alien planet with a TV in its tummy ______

The prefix ***micro*** means *very small* or *makes bigger or stronger*.

What am I?

4. something you use to look at very small things ______
5. something you use to make sounds louder ______

Read and learn

Read the text below. What do the words in **bold** mean?

> Our teacher showed us how to **search** for pictures on the internet. You **type** the name of what you want to see into a search box. Then lots of **images** come onto the screen. I typed "old computers". Pictures of **enormous** computers came up! I'm **glad** we have much smaller ones now.

Circle the answer closest in meaning to the word in **bold**. The first one has been done for you.

1 **search**	a go	b ask	c look for
2 **type**	a scribble	b write using a computer	c write
3 **images**	a pictures	b stories	c letters
4 **enormous**	a huge	b tiny	c old
5 **glad**	a unhappy	b pleased	c sorry

Puzzle

A text message written on a mobile phone uses shortened words, numbers for words, and so on. This is so it can be written and read quickly. Decode these messages so you can answer the question below.

> **Did u get my msg, Bill?**
>
> Yes thx, Sam. I'd luv to c yr new computer.
> I'll come over L8R 2day.
>
> **Good. Ben will b there 2. Can you come B4 6?**
>
> Sure can. C u then.
>
> **GR8.**

What will Bill and Ben be doing that afternoon?

Your turn to write

The teachers have given everyone in your class an email buddy. Your buddy is called Olly. Send him an email telling him about yourself. Write in a way that is friendly and not too formal.

From:

Subject: Hello

Date:

To: Olly Lang, <ollyl@.newschoolcom.au>

Hi Olly,

My name is

___

___

___

___

___

___

Revise and edit your work. Check the spelling. Make a published copy for your teacher, parent or friend.

Reading for fun

✦ **Which animals talk most on the telephone?**

❖ Yakety-yaks.

✦ **What do you call a computer superhero?**

❖ A screen saver.

✦ **PE Teacher: Why did you kick that ball straight at the school computer?**

❖ Pupil: You told me to put it in the net.

☞ Answers on page 113

15 On display

Quick fun

Find words from the **Topic spelling list** to rhyme with these words. The first one has been done for you.

1. Fact rhymes with act.
2. Ring rhymes with ______.
3. Chance rhymes with ______.
4. Age rhymes with ______.
5. Hearing rhymes with ______.
6. Tapping rhymes with ______.

Topic spelling list

Use the **LOOK-SAY-COVER-WRITE-SAY-CHECK** strategy to learn these words.

pretend	sing	dance
dress-up	costume	curtain
concert	hall	chairs
audience	act	practise
clapping	cheering	display
rumble	acrobat	stage

Use this space to write out your topic words the first time. Use your own paper for extra practice.

Rewrite here those you had the most trouble with.

Spelling strategy

Little words in big words

Some words have other words hidden inside them.
For example: ***play*** has the word ***lay*** inside it. This can help you remember its spelling.

Find a word hidden inside these words. The first one has been done for you.

1. stage stag, tag, age
2. chair ____________
3. practise ____________
4. audience ____________
5. hall ____________
6. acrobat ____________

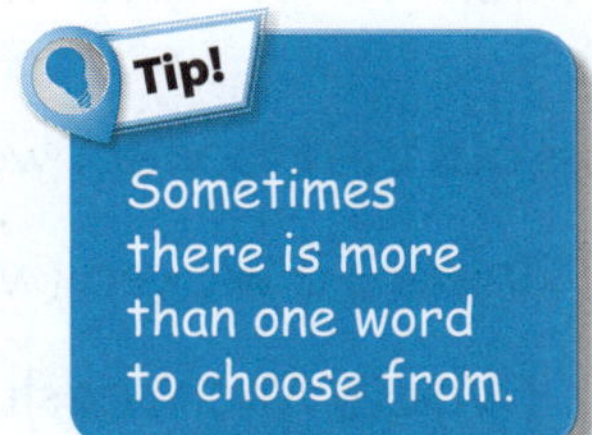

Fill in the gaps

Choose words from the **Topic spelling list** to complete these sentences. The first one has been done for you.

1. There is a display________ of costumes in the library.
2. The a____________ will arrive at 6.00 pm.
3. The c____________ will go up at 6.30 pm.
4. I p____________ to be a witch in our play.
5. My c____________ for the play is a black cloak and a pointy nose.
6. I hope there is c____________ and ch____________ at the end of our play.

Tricky words

The words ***which*** and ***witch*** sound the same but have different meanings and spellings. Think of a way to remember the difference.
For example: a ***witch*** has ***t*** in her middle.

Word	Meaning	Example
which	of what kind?	***Which*** *night is the play on?*
witch	a female who makes magic	*The* ***witch*** *flew off on her broomstick.*

Cross out the incorrect word (*which* or *witch*) in these sentences.

1. There is a wicked (which/witch) in our play.
2. (Which/Witch) costume are you wearing?
3. The concert, (which/witch) is in our hall, is for Year Two.
4. The (which/witch) in *The Wizard of Oz* was scary.

Looking at ... doubling a consonant

If a word has one syllable, one short vowel and one consonant at the end, you double the final consonant when you add a vowel suffix.
For example: *clap* + ***ed*** = **clapped**.

Add the suffix ***ed*** to these words. The first one has been done for you.

1. slap ____slapped____
2. tap ____________
3. stop ____________

Add the suffix ***ing*** to these words.

4. grin ____________
5. hop ____________
6. wrap ____________

Proofreading

Find six spelling mistakes and write the words correctly below. The first one has been done for you.

We made a poster using resycled rubbish.
We used old dres-ups and parts of a broken
chare in our dersplay. Our poster was placed
against the wal for ordiences to view.

1. recycled
2. ______________________
3. ______________________
4. ______________________
5. ______________________
6. ______________________

Vocabulary power

Remember that **prefixes** are letters added to the beginning of a word. Knowing what a prefix means can help with spelling and understanding words.
For example: the prefix ***pre*** means ***before***.

The word prepare is made up of the prefix ***pre*** + pare. To ***prepare*** is to get ready for something before it happens.

Choose a word from the box to complete these sentences. The first one has been done for you.

preschool	predict	prefix
preview	prevent	pretend

1. I will pre vent ______________ that from happening.
2. Pre______________ is where you go before you go to school.
3. Can you pre______________ what will happen in the play?
4. A pre______________ goes at the beginning of a word.
5. We have to pre______________ we are grown-ups today.
6. We watched a pre______________ of the movie on Mum's computer.

Read and learn

Read the text below. What do the words in **bold** mean?

The kids in our street got **together** to make a band. We practise **daily** in a barn at Mick's place. No-one is **over** ten years old in our band. We haven't chosen a name for ourselves **yet**. I **suggested** a name but no-one liked it.

Circle the answer closest in meaning to the word in **bold**. The first one has been done for you.

		a	b	c
1	**together**	a joined	b apart	c with each other
2	**daily**	a often	b twice a day	c every day
3	**over**	a older than	b on top of	c bigger than
4	**yet**	a now	b up to now	c today
5	**suggested**	a described	b had an idea for	c chose

Puzzle

Have fun matching up the authors' names from the box with their play titles.

Willie Catchit	Eva Brick
Rhoda Camel	Justin Tyme
Howard I Know	B Warned
IC Spooks	Norah Bone

1. *The Bus is Coming* by ______________________
2. *Who Stole the Jewels?* by ______________________
3. *Saved by the Bell* by ______________________
4. *Broken Window* by ______________________
5. *Ghosts* by ______________________
6. *Trouble Ahead* by ______________________
7. *Travels in the Desert* by ______________________
8. *The Hungry Dog* by ______________________

Your turn to write

Retell the story of a play or movie you have seen. What happens? How does it end? What is your opinion of it? Did you like it? Why or why not?

Title: ______________________________

____

____

____

____

____

____

____

My opinion:

____

____

Revise and edit your work. Check the spelling. Make a published copy for your teacher, parent or friend.

Reading for fun

✦ **Did you hear about the actor who fell through the floor?**

❖ It was just a stage he was going through.

✦ **Why are movie stars so cool?**

❖ Because they have so many fans.

✦ **What's the problem with twin witches?**

❖ You can't tell which witch is which.

☞ Answers on page 113

Review 3

Now let's see what you remember of the words you learnt in Units 11–15. There are six tests in this review. You could do them all in one session, or you could break them up and do them over a few days.

Step 1 Look at each group of words in the test to revise the spellings.

Step 2 Cover the five words up and test yourself (column 2). Try to do all five words in one go.

Step 3 Write your score out of 5 in the box. If you got any words wrong, go back and study them again.

Step 4 If possible, ask someone to test you on the words later—an hour or even a day later (column 3).

Test 1

Study	Test yourself	Test with another person
after almost often first finally	/5	/5
tomorrow yesterday while Tuesday Wednesday	/5	/5
dislike favourite worst best awful	/5	/5
	Total score = out of 15	Total score = out of 15

Test 2

Study	Test yourself	Test with another person
want prefer fair choose brightest	/5	/5
digging drawing recycling canoeing writing	/5	/5
driving making building noisily quickly	/5	/5
computer mouse decision revision icon	/5	/5
	Total score = out of 20	Total score = out of 20

Test 3

Study	Test yourself	Test with another person
internet email image online website	/5	/5
pretend prevent predict costume curtain	/5	/5
display practise audience chairs acrobat	/5	/5
clapping which where discussion permission	/5	/5
	Total score = out of 20	Total score = out of 20

Test 4

Write the **bold** words correctly. An example has been done for you. Count your score when you have finished the test.

Spelling mistakes	Correct words	Score ✓ ✗
The dog was **diging** for his bone.	digging	
1 We go back to school next **weak**.		
2 Will you carry my **shoping**, please?		
3 I heard a very loud **explotion**.		
4 Have you lost your **citten**?		
5 I'll read my book **wile** I wait for you.		
	Total score	/ 5

Test 5

1 Where does the missing apostrophe (') go in this sentence?
Were going riding with our friends on our bikes today.

○ ○ ○ ○

2 Where does the missing apostrophe (') go in this sentence?
It has rained for weeks and now its starting to snow.

○ ○ ○ ○

3 Which word in this sentence tells how an action is done?
I smiled happily when I saw our new puppy.

○ smiled ○ happily ○ when ○ new

4 Which word in this sentence describes something?
I was excited to wear my black mask in the play.

○ excited ○ wear ○ black ○ play

5 Which word in this sentence has a silent letter?
Last night we saw a full moon in the sky.

○ last ○ night ○ moon ○ sky

Test 6

Underline the word that completes these sentences correctly. An example has been done for you.

Sentences	Score ✓✗
This orange is the (sweet, sweeter, <u>sweetest</u>) of them all.	
1 It will take an (our, hour) to get there.	
2 I rode (quick, quickly) to the shops.	
3 Jupiter is the (large, larger, largest) planet.	
4 That was the (bad, worse, worst) storm I've ever seen.	
5 This is a (good, better, best) bike than that one.	
Total score	/ 5

Grand total	
Test 1	
Test 2	
Test 3	
Test 4	
Test 5	
Test 6	
Total	/ 70

☞ Answers on page 114

Word list

acrobat
act
action
after
alligator
almost
are
athletic
audience
author
awful
bad
baker
ball
bang
bank
barn
beach
before
bend
best
better
black
blue
book
breathe
brightest
brown
building
buses
camping
canoeing
cards
castle
chairs
chapter
cheering
chess
chime
chirp
choose
chuckle
church
circle
city
clapping
cleverly
cloudy
cold
computer
concert
cooking
costume
country
countries
cover
crash
cricket
croak
crocodile
crunch
curtain
curved
cycling
damp
dance
dark
daylight
decision
desert
dessert
digging
difficult
dinosaur
dip
discussion
dislike
display
drawing
dress-up
driver
driving
dry
ear

earholes
early
earth
email
energy
exercising
explosion
famous
fangs
fattest
favourite
finally
first
fizz
flying
font
football
furry
gallery
garden
gardening
gases
gecko
gigantic
glasses
glide
good
green
groan
hairy
hall

hard
hate
hear
helping
hidey
hole
home
hoot
hopscotch
hospital
hot
hour
house
howl
huge
icon
illustrator
image
index
information
internet
island
it's
its
jaws
jigsaw
kindest
kitten
knock
lake
last

late
least
letter
library
lift
like
listen
lizard
look
loudly
love
lumpy
making
mending
mobile
Monday
moon
moonlight
mountain
mouse
move
museum
nearly
need
netball
next
noisily
number
oasis
offices
often

online
orange
our
oval
page
palace
park
permission
picture
pink
plain
plane
planet
planting
playground
practise
predict
prefer
prefix
preschool
press
pretend
prevent
preview
prickly
princesses
print
purple
puzzle
pyramid
quickly
rainbow
rectangle
recycling
red
revision
river
roar
roof
roofs
rough
rounders
rumble
run
running
rustle
Saturn
save
scaly
school
scratchy
screen
search
second
see
selling
shadow
sharp
shell
shelves
shopping
shops
sigh
sing
singing
sizzle
skin
skip
skipping
sky
slide
slimy
slippery
slippery dip
slither
slowly
smell
smooth
snake
Snakes and Ladders
Snap
snarl
sniff
soft
soon
spacecraft
spine
spins
spiral
square
stage
stairs
stare

stars
sticky
story
straight
sunlight
sunny
supermarket
suppose
swim
swing
tag
tail
talk
taste
teacher
telephone
telescope
television
temple
text
their
there
they're
thieves
third
title
today
tomorrow
tonight
tower
town
triangle
trip
Tuesday
turtle
units
valley
velvety
very
village
walk
wall
want
watch
weak
website
Wednesday
week
we're
wet
when
where
which
while
whisper
whistle
white
witch
word
worse
worst
writing
yell
yellow
yesterday
you
yucky
yummy

Answers

1 What can my body do? (pages 2–7)

Quick fun (page 2)
2 look 3 watch 4 hear 5 smell 6 walk

Fill in the gaps (page 3)
2 breathe 3 see 4 run 5 talk 6 whisper

Tricky words (page 4)
1 watch 2 bend 3 lift

Looking at … vowels and consonants (page 4)
2 2 Vs, 3 Cs 3 1 V, 3 Cs 4 2 Vs, 4 Cs 5 3 Vs, 4 Cs

Proofreading (page 5)
2 walk 3 stare 4 see 5 ran

Vocabulary power (page 5)

jump	taste	bend	look
dump	paste	send	cook
bump	waste	mend	took

Read and learn (page 6)
2 c 3 b 4 c 5 a

Puzzle (page 6)
You should have drawn:
1 legs 2 nose 3 eyes 4 hands 5 mouth

2 Plenty of places (pages 8–13)

Quick fun (page 8)
2 country 3 desert 4 home 5 mountain 6 town

Spelling strategy (page 9)
2 ark 3 den 4 is, land, and 5 as, is 6 in

Fill in the gaps (page 9)
2 playground 3 mountain 4 beach 5 supermarket
6 garden

Tricky words (page 10)
1 plain 2 plane 3 plane 4 plain

Looking at … short and long vowels (page 10)
2 long 3 short 4 short 5 long 6 short

Proofreading (page 11)
2 one 3 place 4 visit 5 desert 6 oasis

Vocabulary power (page 11)
Tom: We're going to Bondi Beach. Want to come?
Tim: I can't. Dad is taking us to the city today.
Tom: You mean to Sydney?
Tim: Yes, but tomorrow we are going to Shark Island. Want to come?
Tom: Yes, please!

Read and learn (page 12)
2 b 3 a 4 b 5 c

Puzzle (page 12)
1 e, h, u, s, o
2 house

3 Did you hear that? (pages 14–19)

Quick fun (page 14)
2 hoot 3 fizz 4 knock 5 chirp 6 snarl

Spelling strategy (page 15)
2 howling 3 roaring 4 sizzling 5 chuckling 6 groaning
7 crunching 8 whistling

Fill in the gaps (page 15)
2 roar 3 hoot 4 croak 5 chime 6 rumble

Tricky words (page 16)
1 knock 2 rustle, whistle
3 chalk, write, whale, wheat, kneel

Looking at … short vowel sounds (page 16)
2 bang 3 knock 4 rustle 5 fizz 6 sizzle

Proofreading (page 17)
2 chirp 3 whistle 4 rumbling 5 sound

Vocabulary power (page 17)

Column 1	Column 2
1 whirring	goats
2 exercising	neighbours
3 sizzling	elephants
4 giggling	yaks
5 yowling	wheels
6 noisy	sausages

Read and learn (page 18)
2 b 3 a 4 a 5 c

Puzzle (page 18)

Ssssss	La la la la
Tick tock	Baaaa Baaaaa
Boo hoo	

4 Colours and shapes (pages 20–25)

Quick fun (page 20)
2 pink 3 black 4 blue 5 square 6 straight

Fill in the gaps (page 21)
2 yellow 3 straight 4 circle 5 black 6 triangle

Tricky words (page 22)
1 orange 2 oval 3 square

Looking at … silent letter *e* (page 22)
2 rectangle 3 triangle 4 bundle 5 pale 6 whole

Proofreading (page 23)
2 blue 3 yellow 4 colours 5 trees

Vocabulary power (page 23)

Sentences	Meanings
1 I was caught red-handed with the biscuit tin.	I went pale with shock.
2 I went as white as a sheet.	I looked crossly at him.
3 I was tickled pink with my present.	I'm not getting anywhere.
4 I'm going round in circles.	I was very pleased with my present.
5 I gave him a black look.	I was caught opening the biscuit tin.

Read and learn (page 24)
2 c 3 b 4 a 5 b

Puzzle (page 24)

r	s	w	e	m	w	l
b	t	h	i	p	h	k
l	o	p	d	d	i	s
a	v	u	c	a	t	q
c	i	r	c	l	e	u
k	a	p	l	s	t	a
r	x	l	y	b	e	r
u	r	e	d	a	l	e

5 Reporting on reptiles (pages 26–31)

Quick fun (page 26)
2 turtle 3 snake 4 gecko 5 dinosaur

Fill in the gaps (page 27)
2 tail 3 scaly 4 swim 5 shell 6 slither

Tricky words (page 28)
1 whole 2 hole 3 hole 4 whole

Looking at … long vowel sounds *a* and *i* (page 28)
Long ***a*** sound jar: snake, make, ate, shape
Long ***i*** sound jar: glide, hide, bite, like

Proofreading (page 29)
2 dinosaurs 3 eggs 4 walked 5 tails 6 building

Vocabulary power (page 29)
2 long 3 cold 4 hard 5 scaly 6 round

Read and learn (page 30)
2 b 3 a 4 a 5 c

Puzzle (page 30)
2 A dinodile is half **dinosaur** and half **crocodile**.
3 A turtosaur is half **turtle** and half **dinosaur**.
4 A gecktle is half **gecko** and half **turtle**.
5 A lizigator is half **lizard** and half **alligator**.

Review 1 (pages 32–35)

Test 4 (page 35)
1 desert 2 plane 3 hole 4 mountain 5 gecko

Test 5 (page 35)
1 h 2 b 3 e 4 t 5 k

Test 6 (page 35)
1 (s)ydney is a capital city.
2 We had a holiday on (k)angaroo (i)sland.
3 Have you seen (u)luru at sunset?
4 My new school is called (p)almer (p)rimary.
5 We live in (a)ustralia.

6 Come and play (pages 36–41)

Quick fun (page 36)
2 cricket 3 football 4 netball 5 rounders 6 tag

Spelling strategy (page 37)
2 one 3 three 4 one 5 two 6 two 7 three 8 two
9 three 10 two

Fill in the gaps (page 37)
2 skipping 3 cricket, rounders 4 running 5 Chess 6 Snap

Tricky words (page 38)
1 We're **2** where **3** where **4** Where **5** we're

Looking at … consonant blends *pl* and *sl* (page 38)
The slippery slime sent them sliding down the slope.
There are plenty of planes to play with at the playground.

Proofreading (page 39)
2 ball **3** play **4** castle **5** slippery **6** hidey

Vocabulary power (page 39)
2 raced **3** touched **4** saved **5** kicked **6** cheered

Read and learn (page 40)
2 a **3** b **4** c **5** b

Puzzle (page 40)
1 tricycle **2** crossroads **3** split level **4** going in circles
5 tea for two **6** stuck in traffic

7 Night and day (pages 42–47)

Quick fun (page 42)
2 moon **3** stars **4** planet **5** rainbow **6** sunlight

Spelling strategy (page 43)
1

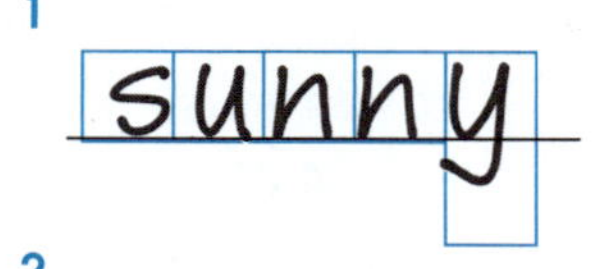

2

3

daylight

Fill in the gaps (page 43)
2 shadow **3** planet **4** spins **5** moon **6** tonight

Tricky words (page 44)
2 rain + bow **3** after + noon **4** day + light
5 space + craft **6** day + time

Looking at … the letters *gh* (page 44)
2 bright **3** light **4** flight **5** might

Proofreading (page 45)
2 night **3** sky **4** see **5** stars **6** planet

Vocabulary power (page 45)

Read and learn (page 46)
2 a **3** c **4** b **5** a

Puzzle (page 46)
Answers should include 6 of the following:

cope	colt	pose	eels
scope	lets	spot	plot
peel	peels	toes	step
pest	pole	lose	close
sleep	slope	slot	

8 From cover to cover (pages 48–53)

Quick fun (page 48)

Fill in the gaps (page 49)
2 story **3** index **4** author **5** library **6** information

Tricky words (page 50)
1 their **2** there **3** Their **4** there

Looking at … *er* endings (page 50)
2 number **3** cover **4** teacher **5** baker **6** driver

Proofreading (page 51)
2 library **3** reptiles **4** story **5** index **6** information

Vocabulary power (page 51)
2 Jack and the Beanstalk
3 Hansel and Gretel
4 The Bunyip of Berkeley's Creek
5 King Kong

6 Alice in Wonderland
7 Tiddalik the Frog

Read and learn (page 52)
2 a 3 c 4 b 5 c

Puzzle (page 52)

9 What's that building? (pages 54–59)

Quick fun (page 54)
2 school 3 church 4 shops 5 tower 6 wall

Spelling strategy (page 55)
1

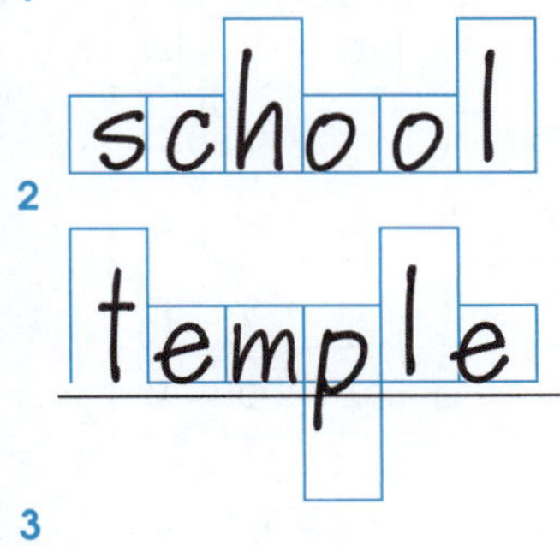

2

3

pyramid

Fill in the gaps (page 55)
2 hospital 3 museum 4 castle 5 wall 6 offices

Looking at … plurals *s*, *ss* and *ies* (page 56)
2 buses 3 kisses 4 babies 5 princesses 6 cities
7 classes 8 countries

Proofreading (page 57)
2 roof 3 church 4 tower 5 hospital 6 stairs

Vocabulary power (page 57)
2 round 3 two 4 interesting, old 5 red 6 new

Read and learn (page 58)
2 b 3 c 4 a 5 b

Puzzle (page 58)

10 How does it feel? (pages 60–65)

Quick fun (page 60)
2 hard 3 sticky 4 dry 5 sharp 6 smooth

Spelling strategy (page 61)
2 one 3 two 4 one 5 two 6 one 7 three

Fill in the gaps (page 61)
2 velvety 3 sticky 4 wet 5 lumpy 6 hairy

Tricky words (page 62)
1 It's 2 its 3 it's 4 its

Looking at … consonant digraphs *th*, *ch* and *sh* (page 62)
2 I cut my thumb on the thick thorn.
3 They thought the bath water was too hot.
4 Chicken pox is very itchy.
5 There is a patch of sticky chewing gum on this bench.
6 That sharp sword makes me shiver and shake.
7 She polished her shiny shoes with a soft brush.

Proofreading (page 63)
2 hairy 3 velvety 4 furry 5 It's 6 its

Vocabulary power (page 63)
2 hotter 3 smoother 4 softer 5 worse 6 wetter

Read and learn (page 64)
2 b 3 b 4 c 5 a

Review 2 (pages 66–69)

Test 4 (page 69)
1 there 2 It's 3 see 4 teacher 5 buses

Test 5 (page 69)
1 one 2 three 3 two 4 one 5 two

Test 6 (page 69)

Column 1	Column 2
1 warm	cloudy
2 rough	dry
3 sunny	light
4 wet	smooth
5 dark	cool

11 Now and then (pages 70–75)

Quick fun (page 70)
2 second 3 third 4 last 5 yesterday 6 today
7 tomorrow

Spelling strategy (page 71)
2 as 3 of, ten 4 at, ate 5 be, for, or, ore 6 fin, all, in

Fill in the gaps (page 71)
2 next 3 before 4 When 5 finally 6 soon

Tricky words (page 72)
1 Weak 2 weak 3 week 4 week

Looking at … trigraphs *tch* and *igh* (page 72)
2 match 3 eye 4 flight 5 scratch

Proofreading (page 73)
2 soon 3 almost 4 running 5 week 6 early

Vocabulary power (page 73)
2 never 3 later 4 now 5 after

Read and learn (page 74)
2 a 3 c 4 a 5 b

Puzzle (page 74)
The message reads:
Hi Jake
I can't meet you now. I can meet you tomorrow at our cubby. See you then.
Jimmy

Reading for fun (page 75)
2 weak/week 3 4 (four)/for; seconds/seconds

12 Likes and dislikes (pages 76–81)

Quick fun (page 76)
2 bad 3 dislike 4 like 5 love 6 worse

Fill in the gaps (page 77)
2 yummy, yucky (or yucky, yummy) 3 best 4 want
5 prefer 6 better

Tricky words (page 78)
1 trip 2 bank 3 fair 4 like

Looking at … words ending with *y* (page 78)
1–5 Answers could include the following:
by, dry, fly, fry, shy, spy, sty, try
6 very 7 yummy 8 yucky

Proofreading (page 79)
2 hope 3 prefers 4 likes 5 very 6 favourite

Vocabulary power (page 79)
2 unkindest 3 ripest 4 sweetest 5 coldest 6 worst

Read and learn (page 80)
2 b 3 c 4 c 5 a

Puzzle (page 80)

y	s	n	g	r	j	x	y	c	h
p	s	h	l	c	y	i	u	n	o
m	g	k	i	h	k	k	w	l	n
e	g	p	k	o	r	l	o	v	e
f	m	l	e	o	k	h	a	l	e
a	b	e	q	s	m	i	e	k	d
w	h	a	t	e	n	f	i	q	d
w	a	n	t	h	n	k	p	w	s
p	r	e	f	e	r	f	n	s	p
l	m	q	n	t	v	u	z	b	k

13 Doing things (pages 82–87)

Quick fun (page 82)
2 drawing 3 driving 4 flying 5 helping 6 making

Spelling strategy (page 83)
2 hard 3 hard 4 soft 5 hard 6 soft

Fill in the gaps (page 83)
2 digging 3 writing 4 building 5 selling 6 canoeing

Tricky words (page 84)
Our class wants everyone at **our** school to recycle drink cans. We spent the lunch **hour** planning how to make this happen. A group of us stayed after school for an **hour** to work on the plan.

Looking at … doubling consonants (page 84)
2 hopping 3 cooking 4 getting 5 knitting 6 gardening

Proofreading (page 85)
2 cycling 3 gardening 4 hour 5 paper 6 doing

Vocabulary power (page 85)
2 (cleverly) 3 (slowly) 4 (noisily) 5 (quickly) 6 (still)

Read and learn (page 86)
2 c 3 b 4 c 5 b

Puzzle (page 86)
Answers should include at least seven of the following: ragged, ring, nine, dine, grade, drag, rage, garden, ride, near

14 Tech talk (pages 88–93)

Quick fun (page 88)
2 website 3 screen 4 telephone 5 mouse 6 computer

Fill in the gaps (page 89)
2 internet 3 icon 4 mobile 5 website 6 email

Tricky words (page 90)
1 screen 2 print
3 small furry animal; object you use with a computer
4 telephone; hanging decoration; moves easily

Looking at … words ending with *sion* (page 90)
2 explosion 3 discussion 4 decision 5 revision

Proofreading (page 91)
2 search 3 telephone 4 found 5 its 6 saved

Vocabulary power (page 91)
1 telephone 2 telescope 3 Teletubby 4 microscope 5 microphone

Read and learn (page 92)
2 b 3 a 4 a 5 b

Puzzle (page 92)
Bill and Ben will be at Sam's place before 6 o'clock to see his new computer.

15 On display (pages 94–99)

Quick fun (page 94)
2 sing 3 dance 4 stage 5 cheering 6 clapping

Spelling strategy (page 95)
2 hair/air 3 act/is 4 die 5 all 6 rob/at/bat

Fill in the gaps (page 95)
2 audience 3 curtain 4 pretend 5 costume 6 clapping, cheering

Tricky words (page 96)
1 witch 2 Which 3 which 4 witch

Looking at … doubling a consonant when adding a suffix (page 96)
2 tapped 3 stopped 4 grinning 5 hopping 6 wrapping

Proofreading (page 97)
2 dress-ups 3 chair 4 display 5 wall 6 audiences

Vocabulary power (page 97)
2 Preschool 3 predict 4 prefix 5 pretend 6 preview

Read and learn (page 98)
2 c 3 a 4 b 5 b

Puzzle (page 98)
1 *The Bus is Coming* by Willie Catchitt
2 *Who Stole the Jewels?* by Howard I Know
3 *Saved by the Bell* by Justin Tyme
4 *Broken Window* by Eva Brick
5 *Ghosts* by IC Spooks
6 *Trouble Ahead* by B Warned
7 *Travels in the Desert* by Rhoda Camel
8 *The Hungry Dog* by Norah Bone

Review 3 (pages 100–103)

Test 4 (page 103)
1 week 2 shopping 3 explosion 4 kitten 5 while

Test 5 (page 103)
1 We're 2 it's 3 happily 4 black 5 night

Test 6 (page 103)
1 hour 2 quickly 3 largest 4 worst 5 better

Notes

Notes

Notes